Apostolic Breakthrough

APOSTOLIC BREAKTHROUGH

Apostolic Breakthrough
Second Edition

Birthing God's Purposes

By Bill Vincent

APOSTOLIC BREAKTHROUGH

© 2016 by Bill Vincent.
All rights reserved. No part of this book may be reproduced, stored in a retrieval system or transmitted in any form or by any means without the prior written permission of the publishers, except by a reviewer who may quote brief passages in a review to be printed in a newspaper, magazine or journal.

Revival Waves of Glory Books & Publishing has allowed this work to remain exactly as the author intended, verbatim, without editorial input.

All Scripture quotations are from the Authorized King James Version of the Bible unless otherwise noted.

Softcover: 978-1542491266

PUBLISHED BY REVIVAL WAVES OF GLORY BOOKS & PUBLISHING
www.revivalwavesofgloryministries.com
Litchfield, IL

Published in the United States of America

Table of Contents

Book Disclaimer 6
True Apostolic 7
The Glory Cloud is Moving 16
Birthing God's Purposes 22
Restoration of Your Soul 30
Transition 37
Prophetic Decrees 55
Living a Life of Victory 88
Supernatural Favor 104
Financial Breakthrough 119
Dreams of God 122
God Alliances 133
Changing Seasons 141
Breakthrough Revival 167
Birthing God's Champions 176
Apostolic Revolution 185
Apostolic Breakthrough Decrees 215
Great Grace 244
About the Author 264
Recommended Books 267

Book Disclaimer

Here are tips on reading Bill Vincent's books. Bill writes prophetically as God speaks. The grammar may be pushed but the message is spoken from the heart of God. Bill didn't want to lose the depth of revelation through extensive editing. God repeats Himself and says things many different ways. If you want to hear prophetically then Bill's the Author for you.

True Apostolic

This is a great way to start this book. There are breakthrough leaders with a Apostolic anointing. LEADERS are being prepared for this next season of the spirit. These mature and loyal prophets will stand before leaders and announce with great power and strength that position changes are coming. It is time for true Apostles to come forth in power. As I began to type this sermon I heard a voice of ultimate authority echo from Heaven, "True Apostolic IS Coming." I received a prophetic word months ago saying, Apostle come forth. Little did I know what was going to be required of me? "We had better get a good understanding of apostolic ministry under us... for it will be on top of us before we know it. Samuel is a type of this apostolic leadership. The Lord did let none of his words fall to the ground nor did he beg his bread from the people."

In this the Lord is indicating valuable attributes in the life and ministry of the prophet Samuel depicting qualities He desires to impart to the apostolic leadership soon to emerge. Careful study in the life of Samuel will provide key secrets to help us qualify for this leadership and touch the heart of the Father in our preparation. In the scriptures, when the Holy Spirit descended upon the Lord to take up His residence in Him, a voice descended from Heaven as an affirmation of this great reality.

Luke 3:22 And the Holy Ghost descended in a bodily shape like a dove upon him, and a voice came from heaven, which said, Thou art my beloved Son; in thee I am well pleased. Likewise, when the disciples witnessed the Lord's transfiguration, they also heard the affirming voice declaring Him to be the Son of God whose words were eternal. The attesting voice from Heaven seems to indicate a truth that is established with certainty to be readily accepted. The apostolic is coming and the better understanding we have of it the more likely we will be to sustain this awesome ministry without being overcome by the intensity and power of it. Let us pray that we can faithfully administer this notable responsibility with character and integrity.

The Lord did let none of Samuel's words fall to the ground. What a profound indication of

Intimacy and relationship between the Lord and His leadership. And Samuel grew and the Lord was with him and did let none of his words fall to the ground.

1 Samuel 3:19 And Samuel grew, and the LORD was with him, and did let none of his words fall to the ground. We must likewise be so intimate with the Lord that we say nothing in His name but what we have received by "a revelation of Jesus Christ."

Galatians 1:12 For I neither received it of man, neither was I taught *it,* but by the revelation of Jesus Christ. Samuel did not speak in the name of the Lord presumptuously or carelessly. Therefore, the Lord was able to perfectly support the words he spoke to the people in the name of the Lord.

The scriptures describe the Lord, our ultimate example, as being so yielded to the Holy Spirit that he said nothing but what he heard from the Father and did nothing but what he saw the Father doing. Do you not believe that I am in the Father and the Father is in me? The words that I say to you I do not speak on my own initiative, but the Father abiding in me does His works.

John 14:10 Believest thou not that I am in the Father, and the Father in me? The words that I speak unto you I speak not of myself: but the Father that dwelleth in me, he doeth the works. We can likewise abide in such a place of surrender to the Holy Spirit that He would let none of our words "fall to the ground" because we would not speak in His name unless we first heard from Him. For all who are being led by the Spirit of God, these are sons of God.

Romans 8:14 For as many as are led by the Spirit of God, they are the sons of God. The Holy Spirit abiding in us will do the same works through us that He did in the Lord.

John 14:12 Verily, verily, I say unto you, He that believeth on me, the works that I do shall he do also; and greater *works* than these shall he do; because I go unto my Father.

One of the most notable attributes in the life of Samuel is his determination not to abuse his position and privileges before God and the people. There was not one person in all of Israel who could bear witness against Samuel for pleading for money, possessions or property. Neither did he allow the spirit of this world to affect his ability to judge the people in righteousness and equity. The apostolic leadership soon to emerge should likewise be characterized by humility and genuine love for the people.

1 Samuel 12:2-4 And now, behold, the king walketh before you: and I am old and grayheaded; and, behold, my sons *are* with you: and I have walked before you from my childhood unto this day. Behold, here I *am:* witness against me before the LORD, and before his anointed: whose ox have I taken? Or whose ass have I taken? or whom have I defrauded? whom have I oppressed? Or of whose hand have I received *any* bribe to blind mine eyes therewith? and I will restore it you. And they said, Thou hast not defrauded us, nor oppressed us, neither hast thou taken ought of any man's hand.

The Apostle Paul admonished the Church of Corinth and the Church of this day to stand in righteousness to judge the affairs of men with wisdom and truth. To do so we must possess the character of Christ reflected in Samuel to be free from the tendency to abuse the anointing and authority of God for unrighteous gain. Certainly, there is a place for giving and supporting the work of the ministry and sharing in the fruitful labors of the anointing. This is an issue of the heart and like Paul we must pray to be trustworthy stewards of the mysteries, power and provisions of God. The prosperity coming to the church will be for kingdom purposes not personal luxury and extravagance. The apostolic church in the book of Acts shared all things in common and delegated resources according to need, reflecting love and unity.

Like Samuel, the anointed leadership the Lord desires to bring to His church will stand before Him as His spokesmen extracting the precious from the profane.

Psalms 99:6, 7 Moses and Aaron among his priests, and Samuel among them that call upon his name; they called upon the LORD, and he answered them. He spake unto them in the cloudy pillar: they kept his testimonies, and the ordinance *that* he gave them.

The ministry of Samuel was established by the Lord's manifest presence in the order of Moses and Aaron, as priests, they were charged with the role of intercession on behalf of God's people and instruction in the ways of righteousness. Faithfulness in these areas will begin to lead the church out of Babylonian confusion and restore her to a place of loyalty and consecration to the Lord. If the Lord can find people without mixture, He will send the Spirit without measure. These faithful leaders were transitional men in covenant relationship with the Lord for transitional times and marked a point of demarcation for the people of God. This perfectly illustrates the nature of the Apostolic leadership the Lord will use in this day. These three represent the Priests, Prophet and Judge (Kingly) anointing that will be entrusted to this maturing leadership. To each of these three, God proved Himself in Mercy and in Judgment.

The coming apostolic ministers will be as a pillar of cloud by day with prophetic anointing that will function as a pillar of fire by night giving illumination. Each will provide a canopy of protection through the Holy Spirit even as Israel was protected during the judgments of Egypt. The shelter of Goshen will become apparent in the coming season. The Lord will allow nothing to come upon the earth unless He first reveals His secret counsel to His servants.

Amos 3:7 Surely the Lord GOD will do nothing, but he revealeth his secret unto his servants the prophets.

Moses, Aaron and Samuel each represent types of the coming government. The manner in which the Lord used these men will also portray the coming leadership and God's dealings with them. He is going to give divinely granted understanding. The scriptures declare that the breath of God gives understanding. He is going to breath upon us to give comprehension of these times and the things we must do to walk intimately with Him as His habitation.

Even though Samuel was born through covenant relationship with incredible destiny, he did not experience the supernatural dealings of God until his prophetic commissioning. Now, Samuel did not yet know the LORD, neither was the word of the LORD yet revealed unto him.

1 Samuel 3:7 Now Samuel did not yet know the LORD, neither was the word of the LORD yet revealed unto him.

There may be many who feel as though they do not qualify for this type of leadership because they have not had prophetic or supernatural experiences in their life. However, the scriptures make it plain; the word of the Lord had not appeared to Samuel until a very specific commissioning experience released him into his purpose and calling. Many of today's "Samuel" type leadership have been hidden and unfamiliar with the visions and revelations of the Lord. Nonetheless, great and profound expressions of the Spirit are imminently awaiting these leaders once the grooming is complete and the timing is appropriate for their release.

The Glory Cloud is Moving

God is releasing revelations like never before and we must move when He moves. I love it when God confirms His word! I was told in a vision to turn to a certain chapter of the Bible and begin to read. After reading several verses in this passage I came upon a "Scripture" that simply said, "increase, increase, increase, increase, increase." Obviously, there is no passage of Scripture that says this precisely, but it was a symbolic representation of God's desire to release escalating measures of increase for the coming days. The passage that I was reading was from Numbers 10. Admittedly, Numbers was not a book that has been on my radar in recent days. I have focused much of my attention on Revelations, Daniel, Zechariah and the Gospel of John. Therefore it was a seemingly random and obscure passage for me to read at the time, yet I knew the vision was from the Lord. As a result, I determined not to tell anyone the specific passage that I was given so when the confirmation came I could have complete confidence that it was from the Lord. In Numbers 10:1-2 and the declaration given to Israel for the purpose of calling a holy assembly and alerting the people for times of movement.

Numbers 10:1, 2 And the LORD spake unto Moses, saying, Make thee two trumpets of silver; of a whole piece shalt thou make them: that thou mayest use them for the calling of the assembly, and for the journeying of the camps.

Numbers 10 is a chapter devoted to the preparation of God's people to move with the cloud of His presence into a place of promise. Very specific and meticulous instruction was given to Moses when the time came for the cloud to move to another location. Clearly, from this prophetic insight, the body of Christ is being called to a holy assembly and preparing to follow the movement of His presence.

The specific verse that I was reading in my VISION that was translated "increase, increase, increase, increase, increase" was actually Numbers 10:28 saying,

Numbers 10:28 Thus *were* the journeyings of the children of Israel according to their armies, when they set forward.

My interpretation of this passage as it relates to the coming increase is derived from our necessity to follow God's meticulous order outlined by His Spirit. The Lord has a prescribed way that He desires for us to align ourselves with Him in order for His blessings of favor and grace to accompany us, resulting in progressive measures of increase.

Much of that order can be found in,
Isaiah 66:1, 2 Thus saith the LORD, The heaven *is* my throne, and the earth *is* my footstool: where *is* the house that ye build unto me? and where *is* the place of my rest? For all those *things* hath mine hand made, and all those *things* have been, saith the LORD: but to this *man* will I look, *even* to *him that is* poor and of a contrite spirit, and trembleth at my word. Three things will help align us with God for the coming days: The Spirit of Humility A Broken and Contrite Heart Trembling in Reverence and Awe at God's Word (Rhema & Logos)

The Lord clearly instructed Moses to have three tribes precede the Tabernacle as they began to march Judah, Issachar and Zebulun.

Numbers 10:14-16 In the first *place* went the standard of the camp of the children of Judah according to their armies: and over his host *was* Nahshon the son of Amminadab. And over the host of the tribe of the children of Issachar *was* Nethaneel the son of Zuar. And over the host of the tribe of the children of Zebulun *was* Eliab the son of Helon.

The standard representing Judah was that of a lion. Clearly, the Lord is presenting Himself as the Lion from the tribe of Judah. He came once in a manger and offered Himself as a suffering lamb. However, now He comes roaring in resurrection power to appropriate His overcoming victory through a body of people identified as the Bride of Christ praise must go before us along with a clear understanding of times and seasons as depicted in the blessings of Issachar. We are now entering an "appointed time" for advancement and especially the recovery of lost heritage. While in South Africa following Rosh Hashanah very clear revelatory insights were given concerning Zebulun and the blessing of Moses found in Deuteronomy 33:18-19.

Deuteronomy 33:18, 19 And of Zebulun he said, Rejoice, Zebulun, in thy going out; and, Issachar, in thy tents. They shall call the people unto the mountain; there they shall offer sacrifices of righteousness: for they shall suck *of* the abundance of the seas, and *of* treasures hid in the sand.

The name Zebulun means "a habitation" but the land of Zebulun was once ostracized for its darkness and apostasy. However, one visitation from the Lord Jesus and it became known as a land of illumination and a source of great light.

Matthew 4:15, 16 The land of Zabulon, and the land of Nephthalim, *by* the way of the sea, beyond Jordan, Galilee of the Gentiles; The people which sat in darkness saw great light; and to them which sat in the region and shadow of death light is sprung up.

This Blessing provides a prophetic picture of many places being positioned for divine visitation. I believe this will be especially true along certain coastal areas that have received prophetic promises through the blessings of Zebulun. Naturally, that is not to say this will be limited to coastal areas but this word is identifying those places with its promise.

I believe this past fall festival season has been one of the most important in recent memory. Clear and precise revelations have been granted concerning God's desire to release not only demonstrations of His spirit but also a more pronounced measure of His presence. We are called and commissioned in this season to bring in a wave of harvest that will consist of future harvesters; the cloud is moving in that direction. Along with our emphasis on evangelism there must also be a corresponding emphasis on equipping, mentoring and preparation.

Birthing God's Purposes

There are seeds that have been sown for hundreds of years and now are the time to birth those seeds. It is time to birth all that God has for us. Are you really ready for some breakthrough in your life, family and ministry?

Isaiah 6:9, 10 And he said, Go, and tell this people, Hear ye indeed, but understand not; and see ye indeed, but perceive not. Make the heart of this people fat, and make their ears heavy, and shut their eyes; lest they see with their eyes, and hear with their ears, and understand with their heart, and convert, and be healed. I prophetically spoke this in the midst of revival. This did not seem to be a word of great encouragement.

Who would want a prophetic word declaring their eyes to be dim and their ears dull unless they should see and hear the day of their visitation and return to the Lord and be healed?

Matthew 13:11-16 He answered and said unto them, Because it is given unto you to know the mysteries of the kingdom of heaven, but to them it is not given. For whosoever hath, to him shall be given, and he shall have more abundance: but whosoever hath not, from him shall be taken away even that he hath. Therefore speak I to them in parables: because they seeing see not; and hearing they hear not, neither do they understand. And in them is fulfilled the prophecy of Esaias, which saith, By hearing ye shall hear, and shall not understand; and seeing ye shall see, and shall not perceive: For this people's heart is waxed gross, and *their* ears are dull of hearing, and their eyes they have closed; lest at any time they should see with *their* eyes, and hear with *their* ears, and should understand with *their* heart, and should be converted, and I should heal them. But blessed *are* your eyes, for they see: and your ears, for they hear.

Isaiah 6 clearly prophesies the spirit of revelation that is necessary to illumine our eyes and ears, this was withheld from that generation of people in order that they could not recognize the day of their visitation. The scriptures point out, if they had then they would have surely returned to the Lord and he would be required, according to His promise, to heal them. Thankfully, we have the biblical pledge that we do not have to remain in such a condition. Although Isaiah rightly prophesied concerning a generation whose ears were dull and whose eyes were dim and unable to recognize the day of their visitation. We have the revelatory assurance that....To us it has been granted to know the mysteries of the kingdom.

It is our right, prerogative and admonition to be anointed with the spirit of revelation that our eyes would be illumined and our ears unstopped that we might know and understand the mysteries of the kingdom. In other words, we have the right to be anointed with the spirit of revelation which brings insight to us concerning the mind, will and purpose of God in the earth and the unveiling of His kingdom. One of the things most adamantly opposed by the enemy is the full release of this spirit upon the church. Our adversary knows that God's people are anointed with the prophetic mandate to be clothed with revelation, then we would return to the Lord and He would have to heal us. That healing would not merely consist of physical and emotional restoration, but also fully mending the breach that has existed between God and man since the Garden of Eden.

Once accomplished, the reality of "CHRIST IN US THE HOPE OF GLORY" becomes apparent and we walk in the prophetic destiny foretold in the scriptures. That is the reason there has been so much opposition to the emerging prophetic generation.

Ephesians 1:17-19 emphasizes the right of every believer to be anointed with the spirit of wisdom and revelation. This form of wisdom is not merely the ability to mentally analyze a situation and make a good response. Rather, it is a spiritual endowment that allows us to go deep into the heart of the Father to see and understand the mysteries of the kingdom and our rights through redemption. Not only do we have the right to understand these mysteries but also the right to the accompanying spirit and revelation which gives illumination and comprehension of their reality.

Ephesians 1:17-19 That the God of our Lord Jesus Christ, the Father of glory, may give unto you the spirit of wisdom and revelation in the knowledge of him: The eyes of your understanding being enlightened; that ye may know what is the hope of his calling, and what the riches of the glory of his inheritance in the saints, And what *is* the exceeding greatness of his power to us-ward who believe, according to the working of his mighty power, The spirit of wisdom is more clearly defined as a supernatural impartation of the spirit granting the ability to see and recognize the Lord Jesus with a spiritual knowledge and comprehension of His mysteries, plans and purposes. This heritage will reveal the manifold and unsearchable wisdom and secrets of God that are hidden in Christ. It relates to a deeper intimacy and awareness into the things of God and invites a personal close encounter with the Lord. The accompanying spirit of revelation grants a comprehension of these mysteries and attributes of God. It involves an understanding and perception with our soul of these things revealed in the spirit. It grants us the ability to not only know the things of God but also the practical application of them in the earth and in our lives. True Apostle Paul was anointed and flowed with this spirit as he continually conveyed the mysteries of the kingdom to his generation. This same spirit is essential for us in this generation to know the concealed secrets reserved for the last days and share in the hidden manna set aside for the end-time perfecting of the bride.

Daniel 12:4 But thou, O Daniel, shut up the words, and seal the book, *even* to the time of the end: many shall run to and fro, and knowledge shall be increased.

According to Ephesians 1:18-19, it provides three blessings essential for our ability to walk in the full measure of Christ through the eyes of our heart being enlightened. That we may know what is the hope of His calling. What are the riches of the glory of His inheritance in the saints? What is the surpassing greatness of His power toward us who believe? When we read these words our minds recognize the great promise that has been provided to us. Even so, when anointed with the spirit of wisdom and revelation, we begin to obtain a comprehension experientially of the reality of this redemptive birthright. As the scriptures point out, eye has not seen, ear has not heard nor has it entered into the heart of man all the great blessings the Lord has provided for us. These must be revealed by the spirit.

To us it has been granted. That is the emphasis of the spirit for this particular time the body at large...To fully apprehend this exceptional mystery. To us it has been granted in this generation to be anointed with the spirit of revelation to know and comprehend these great mysteries provided for us through the awesome power of redemption. One of the greatest mysteries that will be fully realized is the wonder of Christ in us the Hope of Glory. We recite the words but very few experientially discover the absolute and complete reality. However, we believe the scriptures have promised that an entire company of believers will soon emerge anointed with this certainty, walking in the fullness of it with great power and authority and more importantly, radiating the nature and character of Christ through His manifested Glory. It is especially noteworthy that the full revelation required the joining together of the minstrel and prophetic mantle. This in itself depicts the emerging partnership between worship and the prophetic, giving full expression to the heart of the spirit. Elisha was clearly able to more readily discern the voice of God as the minstrel played providing an atmosphere for the prophetic voice to flourish. I believe this will amplify in time with some services allowing the worshipers to continue as the anointed word flows through the prophetic leaders bringing the Word of the Lord in unison with the overflow of minstrel worship.

Restoration of Your Soul

Many times our biggest breakthroughs needed are those things inside of our souls. I personally have experienced a time of God restoring my soul. I had a full team of ministry that for the most part turned their back on me. This was after a controversial way God had me step away from a Revival that was ongoing for over two years. I promise you that we have a God that will love us and restore our soul.

Job 33:29, 30 Lo, all these *things* worketh God oftentimes with man, To bring back his soul from the pit, to be enlightened with the light of the living.

Psalms 23:3 He restoreth my soul: he leadeth me in the paths of righteousness for his name's sake.

The Apostle Paul under the inspiration of the Holy Spirit once wrote to the church in Thessalonica his prayer that the God of peace would sanctify them entirely and preserve their SPIRIT, SOUL and BODY completely and without blame. The power of redemption is provided to not only sanctify our spirit but also our soul and our body. Presently, the spotlight of the Lord is on the soul of man reflecting His desire for total dominion in every department of life so that our fellowship with Him would be unhindered by the corruption of the carnal nature. The Lord's desire is for the restoration of the soul returning to the place of harmonious communion with God that was lost in the Garden of Eden with the fall of man. The soul is identified as the mind, will and emotions of man, the seat of our feelings, desires and affections.

Galatians 5:19-21 Now the works of the flesh are manifest, which are *these;* Adultery, fornication, uncleanness, lasciviousness, Idolatry, witchcraft, hatred, variance, emulations, wrath, strife, seditions, heresies, Envyings, murders, drunkenness, revellings, and such like: of the which I tell you before, as I have also told *you* in time past, that they which do such things shall not inherit the kingdom of God. The scriptures declare that the veil of the temple was rent from top to bottom through the sacrificial offering of the Lord's body. Therefore, if we are not seeing the Lord clearly it is because the veils remain over OUR soul. It is through the "water of the word" that the issues of our soul are exposed and sanctified.

Psalms 18:28 For thou wilt light my candle: the LORD my God will enlighten my darkness. For the word of God is living and active and sharper than any two-edged sword and piercing as far as the division of soul an spirit, of both joints and marrow and able to judge the thoughts and intentions of the heart.

The great patriarch Abraham even experienced this purging process of his soul for complete union with his God. After the promise had been fulfilled and Isaac was born, the scriptures make it clear that Abraham loved his son with a great love. So great was this love for Isaac that it actually became an idol obtaining a position in Abraham rightfully belonging to God? Abraham was then required to demonstrate the complete dedication of his soul to God by willingly submitting the life of Isaac to the Lord. Upon the successful completion of this test, Abraham was able to worship God on an elevated level that he would not have known otherwise. Very often, Isaac is symbolic of our ministry that we sometimes allow to occupy a place of preeminence belonging only to God. Though this purging process is painful, it is necessary to become one spirit with Christ.

It is the literal fulfillment of,
Galatians 2:20 I am crucified with Christ: nevertheless I live; yet not I, but Christ liveth in me: and the life which I now live in the flesh I live by the faith of the Son of God, who loved me, and gave himself for me.

Alexander Dowie was a powerfully anointed leader. He was wonderfully used of the Lord in the ministry of healing and was a prolific writer of scriptural truth. His periodical, "Leaves of Healing" went to an international audience introducing the power of God to the universal church. Unfortunately, Brother Dowie is remembered more for the "Elijah proclamation" than for the awesome ways in which he was used by the Holy Spirit in his generation. Brother Dowie records in his journal that two men requested an audience with him to share the word they reportedly had received from the Lord. During the meeting, these Christian men prophesied to Brother Dowie that they had received a revelation disclosing that Brother Dowie was the prophesied Elijah. Clearly, these men were deceived. Alexander Dowie was so upset with their words that he expelled them from his office immediately. However, Dowie further records that their words were like a hook embedded in his heart. No matter how earnestly he tried, Brother Dowie was unable to free himself from the weight of this proclamation. In the years that followed, the demonically inspired lie grew within his soul until Dowie proclaimed himself the prophesied Elijah. How could such a tragic thing happen to a precious man of God wonderfully used by the Holy Spirit? Even in Brother Dowie's case, the Lord desired to deal with Him and was unable to extract for reasons known only to God. This left opportunity to the enemy to exploit those seeds of corruption resulting in spiritual error. The Lord is now giving us the divine opportunity to allow his spirit to purge and extract from us every tendency toward corruption becoming partaker's of the divine nature free from the corruption of this world and its lusts.

In John 14:30 the Lord announced that satan was coming to him, yet he (satan) had no place in the Lord. In other words, there were no seeds of corruption to exploit in the Lord's nature. Temptation only has power when there are some principles residing in us which are in accord with the designs of the tempter and which may be stimulated by presenting corresponding objects until our virtue is overcome. Where there is no such propensity, temptation has no power. Many things can be allowed to occupy the thrones of our soul and will vary with each individual. However, each can be traced to the carnal nature of man and the elevation of "self". A glorious opportunity is being offered to those willing to pay the price and experience this purging process for the joy of perfect fellowship after its completion. We should each pray that the Holy Spirit will reveal to us areas of our soul remaining subject to the carnal nature. Through repentance and the yielding of our will, He will then extract worldly passions and impart the divine nature. We are given the magnificent opportunity to come to the Lord and take His yoke upon us AND FIND REST FOR OUR SOULS. Seeing that His divine power has granted to us everything pertaining to life and godliness, through the true knowledge of Him who called us by His own glory and excellence. For by these He has granted to us His precious and magnificent promises, in order that by them you might become partakers of the divine nature, having escaped the corruption that is in the world by lust.

2 Peter 1:3, 4 According as his divine power hath given unto us all things that *pertain* unto life and godliness, through the knowledge of him that hath called us to glory and virtue: Whereby are given unto us exceeding great and precious promises: that by these ye might be partakers of the divine nature, having escaped the corruption that is in the world through lust.

Transition

Transition is more than a topic, it's a movement. God takes us out of the old into the new. I taught on this topic for over six hours that will help everyone going through a transition. I am going to reveal a crucial key for successfully going through times of transition. You will come to understand the importance of consecration, staying in the Secret Place and why your sanctification is vital to the release of God's marvels in the earth. Then, you will learn how your intimacy with God not only affects you, but it also affects the nations. I will explain, by drawing from the life of Moses, how God's presence is released upon our lives, how His glory manifests and what hinders God's glory from being revealed. Right now, like so many Christians, you are probably smack-dab right in the middle of a change of seasons, spiritually speaking! What was familiar may no longer be in sight and you might even be feeling a little shaky on your feet. So it's vital not to lose sight of God. The Lord is there for you, always and He'll strengthen you and show you the way to go.

Hebrews 13:5 *Let your* conversation *be* without covetousness; *and be* content with such things as ye have: for he hath said, I will never leave thee, nor forsake thee.

Psalms 119:105 Thy word *is* a lamp unto my feet, and a light unto my path.

In fact, if you're in a transition, the good news is you are actually heading somewhere, a certain destination, because transition means: passage from one state, style or place to another! Still, to make sure you don't end up just going around in circles, God wants to place a "spiritual compass" in your hand. That compass is "wired" to point you off in the right direction straight to the Father's heart the Secret Place. That special place is where we love on God, get our bearings, grow in our relationship and walk with Him and get strengthened and filled. Therefore, in this chapter my goal is to help establish your spiritual footing through times of transition by checking the "compass" and taking you to the secret place. To get there we're going to journey together to key places like consecration, the importance of staying in the secret place and the benefits of sanctification. So let's go now to the ancient book of Leviticus, beginning at chapter 8.

Leviticus 8:33-35 And ye shall not go out of the door of the tabernacle of the congregation *in* seven days, until the days of your consecration be at an end: for seven days shall he consecrate you. As he hath done this day, *so* the LORD hath commanded to do, to make an atonement for you. Therefore shall ye abide *at* the door of the tabernacle of the congregation day and night seven days, and keep the charge of the LORD, that ye die not: for so I am commanded.

The meaning of the number seven in scripture is completion and perfection. There was something important that God wanted to accomplish in the hearts of Aaron and his sons during those seven days of consecration. This serious time was absolutely necessary in order to prepare them completely for their priestly ministry on the eighth day. Eight means new beginnings and on that set day Aaron had certain holy practices to complete that also involved his two sons. God had promised to appear to them and the people afterward and scripture says that the glory of the LORD appeared to all the people and fire came out from before the LORD and consumed the burnt offering and the fat on the altar. So, after a time of sacrifice, death and offerings came seven days of consecration to the Lord.

God will bring about His fire, purging and discipline or what I call suffering, for seven days which means until He gets the job done. Until it's complete and perfect, the process will go on. In fact I believe that we can turn a 40-day purpose into 40 years depending on how we respond when the fire begins to fall. Their time of consecration was also like a time of suffering, but with it came the promise of God's glory. There is a profound sweetness found in suffering,
Romans 8:17, 18 And if children, then heirs; heirs of God, and joint-heirs with Christ; if so be that we suffer with *him,* that we may be also glorified together. For I reckon that the sufferings of this present time *are* not worthy *to be compared* with the glory which shall be revealed in us.

I keep seeing this glory that is about to be revealed in the church. But if I can't have the glory without suffering, If I can't get to the new beginnings without seven days of consecration, I would much rather embrace the dealings of God now and judge myself now than be judged later. Just look at what happened to Aaron's two sons. They died after that time of consecration because they brought strange fire before the Lord. Fire came out from the presence of the Lord and consumed them and they died.

With Aaron's two sons now dead, his other two sons were appointed for priestly service to the Lord. Next, Moses told them all,
Leviticus 10:1, 2 And Nadab and Abihu, the sons of Aaron, took either of them his censer, and put fire therein, and put incense thereon, and offered strange fire before the LORD, which he commanded them not. And there went out fire from the LORD, and devoured them, and they died before the LORD.

Remaining in God's presence is of the utmost importance! Why? The answer is because it is the threshold for new beginnings that we might live and much more.

The Bible says that Moses' servant/assistant Joshua, the son of Nun, remained in the tabernacle.

Exodus 33:11 And the LORD spake unto Moses face to face, as a man speaketh unto his friend. And he turned again into the camp: but his servant Joshua, the son of Nun, a young man, departed not out of the tabernacle.

It was Joshua who took the children of Israel across the river Jordan into Promised Land the place of new beginnings! What qualified Joshua to be ready for the next season? It was this: he did not depart from the tabernacle of the Lord. Too many men, ministries, leaders are dying, not literally but spiritually, because the anointing oil of the Lord is upon them and they aren't remaining in the doorway of the "tabernacle," the Secret Place. There is a promise of a new anointing that comes with the new beginning and the new beginning is established for those that come back to the Secret Place and embrace the priestly ministry of worship and the word.

Joshua remained in the tabernacle and he was God's appointed leader for the next season. When the time came for the children of Israel to cross the river Jordan, He told them:

Joshua 3:5 And Joshua said unto the people, Sanctify yourselves: for to morrow the LORD will do wonders among you.

Sanctifying ourselves is vital and integral to God's marvels being released. Sanctification means: to make holy; set apart as sacred; consecrate. Many people want the supernatural, the miracles, signs and wonders and we do need them, don't get me wrong. However, such acts really only have eternal weight and glory through a believer's sanctification to God. Think of what Moses had with God.

God said to Moses:
Exodus 34:10 And he said, Behold, I make a covenant: before all thy people I will do marvels, such as have not been done in all the earth, nor in any nation: and all the people among which thou *art* shall see the work of the LORD: for it *is* a terrible thing that I will do with thee.

Moses was sanctified; his life was set apart for the Lord. And also remember, God made that promise when the Ten Commandments were being written on Mount Sinai commandments for holy living. God made another promise earlier, a covenant promise that He was going to give the land that he swore to Abraham, Isaac and Jacob.

Exodus 33:1 And the LORD said unto Moses, Depart, *and* go up hence, thou and the people which thou hast brought up out of the land of Egypt, unto the land which I sware unto Abraham, to Isaac, and to Jacob, saying, Unto thy seed will I give it:

Have you ever had God say something to you like, "I will give it?" Do you want to enter into the land? I know I do! How many of you want to enter into a time where God will work marvels in the nations such as we've not seen in all the earth so that Jesus can be glorified and the great harvest can come in? God made me a promise about this for the next season. He said, "I will do marvels such as have not been done in all the earth. In all the people among whom you are they shall see the work of the Lord. It is an awesome thing that I will do for you." Right now God is raising the standard and He is offering us as individuals an opportunity to consecrate ourselves in the Secret Place as we embrace going lower so we can go higher in Christ Jesus.

In this place, as shifts and transitions present themselves, they will not dominate our lives negatively but they will drive us into the safety and wisdom of the heart of God. So get ready for the rest of this chapter because we're going to journey to a few more places along the way to the secret place.

I am writing about God's glory, how it is released upon our lives, how it manifests and also what hinders God's glory from manifesting. In order to get to the secret place, last week we journeyed to three key positions: consecration, staying in the secret place and sanctification. I want to continue this chapter by drawing valuable lessons from the life of Moses. Also I want to speak prophetically, later in this chapter, to some of you who are experiencing a time of transition.

True to His Word, God intended to give the nation of Israel their inheritance, their land, but He had to tell the people:

Exodus 33:2, 3 And I will send an angel before thee; and I will drive out the Canaanite, the Amorite, and the Hittite, and the Perizzite, the Hivite, and the Jebusite: Unto a land flowing with milk and honey: for I will not go up in the midst of thee; for thou *art* a stiffnecked people: lest I consume thee in the way.

What Mercy! They were a stiff-necked people but God would send his angel to drive out their enemies. Who wouldn't want that? But look at this. Moses thought: You know what? That's not good enough! The promise of the inheritance is good, even the promise of the angel is good, but I want what's most important God's presence! Church, our challenge is this. Many of us have been satisfied with the angel; there's been lots of activity and miracles and we've been satisfied in that. But then we've drifted out of the tabernacle and left the secret place of His presence, getting burned out, not even realizing we've left the place of intimacy. All the activity has taken priority. We love the prophetic encounters and experiences. But don't camp there! Don't be satisfied with the angels in this hour! Be like Moses who wanted God, Himself! More than anything he wanted God's presence to go with them as they took

the Promised Land. Of course, God answered the cry of Moses! He said,
Exodus 33:14 And he said, My presence shall go *with thee,* and I will give thee rest.

What a victory for Moses! Now why would God give such favor to him (and the nations of Israel)? Part of the answer is because Moses had history with the Lord, a history of intimacy and a relationship that was built up over the years. And so the Lord said to Moses,

Exodus 33:17 And the LORD said unto Moses, I will do this thing also that thou hast spoken: for thou hast found grace in my sight, and I know thee by name.

With this in mind, I want you to understand there is a powerful place in intercession right now. This place is being offered to those that have a history of intimacy with God and for those that have embraced the tabernacle and the friendship of God. There's a scripture that says:
Leviticus 10:7 And ye shall not go out from the door of the tabernacle of the congregation, lest ye die: for the anointing oil of the LORD *is* upon you. And they did according to the word of Moses.

If you are heeding that scripture right now, the place of intercession is for you! God is bringing a new beginning the anointing of the priestly ministry. Only somebody that has a history of intimacy with God can pray the way Moses prayed. On more than one occasion Moses stood in the gap on behalf of his nation and he even turned away God's wrath from coming upon the people.

Exodus 32:11-14 And Moses besought the LORD his God, and said, LORD, why doth thy wrath wax hot against thy people, which thou hast brought forth out of the land of Egypt with great power, and with a mighty hand? Wherefore should the Egyptians speak, and say, For mischief did he bring them out, to slay them in the mountains, and to consume them from the face of the earth? Turn from thy fierce wrath, and repent of this evil against thy people. Remember Abraham, Isaac, and Israel, thy servants, to whom thou swarest by thine own self, and saidst unto them, I will multiply your seed as the stars of heaven, and all this land that I have spoken of will I give unto your seed, and they shall inherit *it* for ever. And the LORD repented of the evil which he thought to do unto his people. He was drawing on, or counting on, his place of friendship and intercession with God, not for his own sake or his own needs. Now think about this. He was concerned about receiving mercy from the Lord for the nation and for God's very presence to go with them. He knew God's presence would distinguish them from all the other surrounding nations.

Exodus 33:16 For wherein shall it be known here that I and thy people have found grace in thy sight? *is it* not in that thou goest with us? so shall we be separated, I and thy people, from all the people that *are* upon the face of the earth.

For those who are in transition in this season, prophetically I want to say that as you abide in the secret place, the tabernacle, God is offering you a powerful place in intercession in which things get done. That's the kind of season God wants to bring you into at this time drawing on your history in Him and interceding for whatever god puts on your heart. Your history with God can affect the world! Like Moses you might be called to stand in intercession for your nation, or it might be other nations in the world; a very important assignment in perilous days such as these.

Right after Moses received God's favor he wasted no time. He wanted to know the inner reality of who is/was and so Moses asked the Lord.

Exodus 33:17, 18 And the LORD said unto Moses, I will do this thing also that thou hast spoken: for thou hast found grace in my sight, and I know thee by name. And he said, I beseech thee, shew me thy glory.

God responded by saying,
Exodus 33:19 And he said, I will make all my goodness pass before thee, and I will proclaim the name of the LORD before thee; and will be gracious to whom I will be gracious, and will shew mercy on whom I will shew mercy.

Now many believers think of God's glory in this context: glory cloud, pillar of cloud, a glory mist, glory liquid honey clouds, gold dust, or diamonds falling from heaven. However, how does the glory of the Lord manifest in this scripture? The answer is: God's goodness! How many of you would like to have a visitation of a season of just God's goodness coming to you? You've asked God to show you the inner reality of who He is and God is your friend so He says, "I will show you the inner reality of who I am. One way I am going to do it is I am going to bring goodness and kindness into your life and ministry because you wanted me more than you wanted the angel."

Back to Moses!

Look at what begins to take place in,
Exodus 33:21, 22 And the LORD said, Behold, *there is* a place by me, and thou shalt stand upon a rock: And it shall come to pass, while my glory passeth by, that I will put thee in a clift of the rock, and will cover thee with my hand while I pass by:

This is important for this hour if we are going to get where God wants us to go, the "cleft of the rock" is the only shelter we have. This is a time of being hidden in Christ, hidden in the cleft of the rock. That spiritual position only happens when we go very low and if we do that, the glory will "pass by" and we'll be able to receive of God's goodness. But only people right now that are getting back to the secret place and hiding in the cleft of the rock are going to be able to receive the goodness that's about to drop from heaven.

Look at what hiding brings,
Exodus 34:5 And the LORD descended in the cloud, and stood with him there, and proclaimed the name of the LORD. This is God, Himself, saying, "Here I am!" Proclaiming Himself. It's a visitation!

Exodus 34:10 And he said, Behold, I make a covenant: before all thy people I will do marvels, such as have not been done in all the earth, nor in any nation: and all the people among which thou *art* shall see the work of the LORD: for it *is* a terrible thing that I will do with thee. If you will embrace the season of hidden-ness, now, visitation will be upon you. hidden-ness brings a personal visitation of the Lord, Himself. It releases the works of the Lord. For your nation, today, don't you want the promise of God's marvels to be manifested? In all the people among whom you are they shall see the work of the Lord. It is an awesome thing that I will do for you. Nothing is impossible for God! So in that hidden place, not being satisfied with just an angel, going on to embrace remaining in the tabernacle, embracing the call to hidden-ness, will release a powerful visitation of the Lord Himself, or what I call a "mighty visitation."

This will release works like we've never seen before. Marvels!

You know, when Moses came down from Mount Sinai with the Ten Commandments he did not know that his face was shining.

Exodus 34:29 And it came to pass, when Moses came down from mount Sinai with the two tables of testimony in Moses' hand, when he came down from the mount, that Moses wist not that the skin of his face shone while he talked with him.

Moses lost sight of himself. He was totally unaware of how much glory was upon him. I believe that the one reason we are not walking in a greater degree of the manifestation of the glory is we are too aware of the glory we have. We are too aware of the gift and the influence that we have. But if we will lose sight of ourselves, there will be a glory that comes that is greater than anything that we've seen. And that can only happen when we empty ourselves and we are consumed with the face of the King and doing what the King has called us to do; and nothings else matters anymore.

We do need a coming revival that has power and that has resurrection in it. But if we, as a church, would get so consumed in being in the presence of the King and in the tabernacle, like Joshua, wanting the inner reality of whom the Lord is, then God will visit us. That visitation will release the wonders and the works that we not only want him to release, but we need him to release because it's the one thing that makes us distinct and different from any other nation and religion. But as I just said, it begins by emptying ourselves. So allow the Holy Spirit to minister to your heart so that your season of change and transition leads you to the tabernacle, the secret place of His presence. In that place you will get your bearings and God will bring you understanding and revelation. You'll see restoration take place in your life and you'll be anointed with fresh oil to press through your transition to breakthrough and victory!

Prophetic Decrees

This Chapter is brought forth from a teaching series that I could never finish. I have preached over three hours and never could finish the teaching. I decided to write a Chapter in this book.

I will help you understand why God gives us prophetic words, visions, revelations and examines and uncovers those things that hinder the fulfillment of God's prophetic word in our lives. Many are missing the mark of their calling and the words that have come to us from God remain unfulfilled. Then we will continue with the quest for success in appropriating what God has promised us. We'll learn how to war for our words and how we can effectively shoot prophetic arrows in the heavens to "scatter the demonic allies." How many prophetic promises and words spoken over your life have you yet to see birthed?

Every believer has prophetic promises from heaven whether God has revealed something that we would accomplish for Him, something that we would become, or something that we would see Him do in our authoritative words that Scripture says we would "do well to pay attention to."

2 Peter 1:19 We have also a more sure word of prophecy; whereunto ye do well that ye take heed, as unto a light that shineth in a dark place, until the day dawn, and the day star arise in your hearts:

Countless believers have waited years to realize the fulfillment of prophetic words spoken over them, or revelations from visitors or dreams. Do you ever wonder what to do with them, how to act upon them, or how to ensure the fulfillment of them in your life or ministry? How do we bring the words of the Lord to pass? What hinders the fulfillment of them?

Some blame the delay on the prophet or the person who delivered the word and others blame themselves. Sadly, many give up believing their promises. However, delay in the fulfillment of a heavenly word spoken over you may have everything to do with the enemy opposing, dark, spiritual forces determined to sabotage your destiny. Then the delay does have something to do with us, for the delay is in our lack of response. We give up waiting or we don't determine that "word" really was for us and give up on the vision. We don't do what God has called us to do because our mindsets aren't in line with the potential God gives us. We're not responding by pulling from heaven "those things that are not as though they were."

There are things that have always been in the eternal purpose of God, it's just that they're not in our natural realm yet. But the promises of God have always been in the Father's heart, even before the foundation of the world. Everything we need in the natural to do what God has called us to do is available in the invisible realm.

We must learn how to see the promises of God in the invisible by the eye of faith, embrace it in the invisible and bring it to the earth. Embrace, confess and declare God's promises into the heavens!

Grab hold of this truth. Prophetic decrees made into the heavens have the power to revolutionize your life! Heavenly prophetic decrees and proclamations hasten the fulfillment of God's word over your life. They're powerful! They thwart the plans of the enemy and accelerate the birth and fulfillment of every prophetic promise and revelation spoken over you! When I learned how to make prophetic decrees and proclamations in my own life, God was able to do a whole lot a whole lot faster in me and through me.

Recently, the Lord showed me that through our prophetic decrees, He also releases angels to battle the forces of the enemy to bring us what is rightfully ours! That's part of their job description! I hope to give some insight in this teaching on how you can make prophetic decrees and proclamations into the heavens, which will hasten and bring to pass the Word of the Lord. I want you to understand your responsibility with God-given promises and visions and how you can partner with God to realize your destiny.

Let's look at a passage in the gospel of Matthew that speaks of our responsibility with the Word of the Lord:
Matthew 16:13-16 When Jesus came into the coasts of Caesarea Philippi, he asked his disciples, saying, Whom do men say that I the

Son of man am? And they said, Some *say that thou art* John the Baptist: some, Elias; and others, Jeremias, or one of the prophets. He saith unto them, But whom say ye that I am? And Simon Peter answered and said, Thou art the Christ, the Son of the living God.

Take note of one thought in this passage: "Peter, flesh and blood has not revealed this to you, but my father who is in heaven." Peter's revelation came from heaven. You may also have received divine inspiration like Peter a prophetic word, a vision or perhaps an illumined scripture from God. Maybe a prophet called you out and prophesied over you or God spoke to you through television, radio or a dream.

Prophetic words and promises are personal, specific to our lives as individuals, our families, or our ministries. They may also be intended for cities, regions, people and nations. They are always in line with the Word, from Genesis through to Revelation. However, I want to focus primarily on those words that God has given to us personally, those rhema words. Rhema words and God's Word are a powerful combination that can activate our divine destiny.

Let's look again at Jesus' next words to Peter in,
Matthew 16:18 And I say also unto thee, That thou art Peter, and upon this rock I will build my church; and the gates of hell shall not prevail against it.

Now what does Jesus mean by the words on this rock? The Catholic Church accepts that phrase to mean Peter and his ministry, while others think it refers to the apostles. However, I don't believe Peter or the apostles are the rock. I believe Jesus is saying, "upon this rock the rock of revelation I am building…upon the rock of being able to hear what your Father in heaven is saying. Flesh and blood has not revealed this unto you. Upon that rock I shall build My church." In the book of Jeremiah, the Bible also tells us that the purpose of the Lord is to build you and not pull you down, plant you and not pluck you up.

Jeremiah 24:6 For I will set mine eyes upon them for good, and I will bring them again to this land: and I will build them, and not pull *them* down; and I will plant them, and not pluck *them* up.

Jeremiah 42:10 If ye will still abide in this land, then will I build you, and not pull *you* down, and I will plant you, and not pluck *you* up: for I repent me of the evil that I have done unto you.

So, when God gives you a heavenly revelation, it's to build you and plant you. It's to build and plant something in you and through you. It's to build, plant, loose, birth and bring to pass His Word with the help of the Holy Ghost. On the other hand, there are some things we have to tear down in the spirit those forces opposing the fulfillment of God's Word.

Matthew 16:19 And I will give unto thee the keys of the kingdom of heaven: and whatsoever thou shalt bind on earth shall be bound in heaven: and whatsoever thou shalt loose on earth shall be loosed in heaven.

Do you know what the keys are? They are every prophetic word that you have, yes, every revelation you have ever received. Some of us in the Body of Christ run around with a keychain full of keys, like a janitor with keys jingling wherever we go. Maybe you have a whole lot of keys on your key chain.

Perhaps you don't even know which one fits which lock! Sure, you used to know, but many of those keys have been there a long time, so long that you don't even know what they're for anymore. Why have fifty keys on your keychain if you only use a few?

Every time we receive a prophetic word, we add a key to our ring it's a key to the kingdom, your kingdom. It's a key to a destiny. It's a key for you to open up the heavens and loose things in heaven so what God said about you in heaven can come to pass on the earth. With that destiny word, you can build or pull down, plant or pluck up and bring the destiny to its fulfillment. That is what we're supposed to be using the keys for. How many keys are you carrying?

Properly learn how to use the keys handed to you through visions, dreams or words from the Lord. That's what Jesus taught Peter. The Lord's message was: "Peter these are keys. I just gave you a key called "revelation". With that key, you have a responsibility to open up the Kingdom of Heaven so that revelation can come to pass". Rest assured that God usually only shows you something He wants you to have now, not fifty years from now. Yes, He has a timetable, but I don't believe His intention is to dangle a carrot on a string in front of your nose! I don't believe He works that way.

Delays often happen not because of "God's timing," or the devil, but because of us. When God speaks to us, He's not asking us to believe that we can. He's trying to change our identity so that we will. When He gives us a prophetic word, it becomes potential. It becomes a desire that He plants in us. It's a key to bring our destiny to pass. We have a responsibility to birth God's prophetic word and promises. When God speaks something for us, He is releasing potential in us; He's giving us a key to unlock that possibility. But we must posture ourselves to realize that potential.

The fulfillment of prophetic words is conditional, in as much as we are required to respond and take certain steps of obedience. I believe that once we get to heaven, we'll discover how much more God had for us in this life that we never realized or saw to fruition. Many Christians wonder why their dreams are not yet fulfilled. They have good intentions, but never walk out what God has for them. God's reason for giving us these revelatory keys is to excite, edify and encourage us to press on toward the mark; they are filled with possibility. Consider Daniel, he had a revelation while he was reading the book of Jeremiah.

Daniel 9:2 In the first year of his reign I Daniel understood by books the number of the years, whereof the word of the LORD came to Jeremiah the prophet, that he would accomplish seventy years in the desolations of Jerusalem.

As he read, God came along, breathed on the Scripture and said, "Daniel, what Jeremiah prophesied about the Babylonian captivity that's your generation. You are about to come out of Babylonian captivity after 70 years". Daniel didn't just proclaim the news; he birthed it through fasting and prayer. He grabbed hold of it, responded and became involved in God's Word.

God said it and so now, he needed to lay hold of what He said. As Daniel, we must also birth these prophetic words of God. It's not a matter of, "Well, God said it, so He's going to do it... His sovereignty will bring it to pass... I'm just going to wait and see". The prophet delivers God's potential for us, why stone the prophet if things don't happen? The purpose of the prophetic is to stir and cause destiny to come alive in you so you'll become passionate about the potential God planted in you. Daniel hears God's promise of release from Babylonian captivity and he says, "Ok, Now I need to do my part. It's not just good enough that God spoke. I need to pray and fast it through." What if he'd said, "We'll, perhaps God didn't really mean anything by this…. I'm not sure it's going to happen. It's not happening! If it was God, it should have happened already! I mean, God said it!" No, Daniel didn't give up he kept praying and after twenty-one days Michael the archangel appeared and (in effect) said, "Daniel, come over here for a minute.

Let me tell you something. God heard you on the first day. But you see… we ran into some opposition in heaven called the Prince of Persia. The enemy didn't want you to receive what God wanted you to have twenty-one days ago, so there was a delay in the spirit."

It's not that the Word wasn't of God. It's not that the prophet was wrong. But there was a delay in the spirit. Think about your prophetic promises there might be some devils today holding back what is rightfully yours. There is a Prince of Persia in the spiritual realm. I want you to know that God heard you the first day. You should have seen the fulfillment five years ago, but it hasn't come yet. It's not God. It's not you. It's the devil resisting your destiny, tying it up in the spirit. If it happened to Daniel, it can happen to us. God had to send Michael to battle through that Prince of the enemy.

Let me tell you something if the devil came against Jesus and against Moses, he is warring against all of God's people. The devil wants to kill every move of God in its infancy. He wants to discourage you right when you get saved or right when you get healed. He wants to try taking God's blessings from you. Back when God's people were captive in Egypt, satan knew something was going on he knew the prophetic words of Joseph and that they would return to the land of which God swore to Abraham, to Isaac and to Jacob.

Genesis 50:24 And Joseph said unto his brethren, I die: and God will surely visit you, and bring you out of this land unto the land which he sware to Abraham, to Isaac, and to Jacob.

So when Moses was born satan said, "We need to issue a decree. We need to kill all the male children under two years old. We are going to kill them." That's when God had to orchestrate the deliverance of baby Moses.

Matthew 2:16 Then Herod, when he saw that he was mocked of the wise men, was exceeding wroth, and sent forth, and slew all the children that were in Bethlehem, and in all the coasts thereof, from two years old and under, according to the time which he had diligently enquired of the wise men.

After that attempt on Moses' life, the devil tried the same tactic on Jesus and according to, Revelations 12:17 And the dragon was wroth with the woman, and went to make war with the remnant of her seed, which keep the commandments of God, and have the testimony of Jesus Christ.

That's you and I! Satan knows that God has a plan for us. Satan has a plan of destruction he is not just going to lie down, roll over and let you be what God wants you to be. He is working overtime to distract you and to delay the fulfillment of your promises. He is working overtime to sideline you or to kill, steal and destroy in your life. Satan has assigned demonic cohorts in the spiritual realm to keep you from finding the revelation of God's will. And when you do find it, he stirs up a whole lot of mess to get you so distracted that you can't really press on.

Philippians 3:14 I press toward the mark for the prize of the high calling of God in Christ Jesus. He is trying to get you into debt and into immoral relationships he'll try anyway he can to mess up your life.

You have a place of destiny which is fully released as you respond, build and plant. How you respond; what you do or don't do with what God gives you, can determine your destiny. God does not change; however, He will adjust His decrees to fit our response. There are decrees and promises He has made that do not change, such as the covenant with Israel and His new covenant with us.

John 6:37-40 All that the Father giveth me shall come to me; and him that cometh to me I will in no wise cast out. For I came down from heaven, not to do mine own will, but the will of him that sent me. And this is the Father's will which hath sent me, that of all which he hath given me I should lose nothing, but should raise it up again at the last day. And this is the will of him that sent me, that every one which seeth the Son, and believeth on him, may have everlasting life: and I will raise him up at the last day.

John 6:44 No man can come to me, except the Father which hath sent me draw him: and I will raise him up at the last day.

There are others that He has adjusted, such as Abraham's plea for Sodom and Gomorrah, and the sparing of Nineveh.

Jonah 3:1-10 And the word of the LORD came unto Jonah the second time, saying, Arise, go unto Nineveh, that great city, and preach unto it the preaching that I bid thee. So Jonah arose, and went unto Nineveh, according to the word of the LORD. Now Nineveh was an exceeding great city of three days' journey. And Jonah began to enter into the city a day's journey, and he cried, and said, Yet forty days, and Nineveh shall be overthrown. So the people of Nineveh believed God, and proclaimed a fast, and put on sackcloth, from the greatest of them even to the least of them. For word came unto the king of Nineveh, and he arose from his throne, and he laid his robe from him, and covered *him* with sackcloth, and sat in ashes. And he caused *it* to be proclaimed and published through Nineveh by the decree of the king and his nobles, saying, Let neither man nor beast, herd nor flock, taste any thing: let them not feed, nor drink water: But let man and beast be covered with sackcloth, and cry mightily unto God: yea, let them turn every one from his evil way, and from the violence that *is* in their hands. Who can tell *if* God will turn and repent, and turn away from his fierce anger, that we perish not? And God saw their works, that they turned from their evil way; and God repented of the evil, that he had said that he would do unto them; and he did *it* not.

God will adjust His responses to us just as we adjust our responses to God's Abraham changed God's mind and so did Jonah. There is a place where you can barter with God. What God said about you is not a guarantee.

Consider the life of Jonah. If it was true that what God says will happen and that we have nothing to do with it, then Jonah would have just rolled over and said, "Well, if God says He's coming down and bringing destruction and judgment to Nineveh, that is too bad for them. God said it so what can I do about it. God said it; it's got to happen!" Actually, Jonah ran from God because He knew that God would restrain His judgment if the people repented and Jonah didn't want that. Eventually Jonah did deliver the word of God in Nineveh and the people repented. God did change His mind. Therefore, the Word must have been dependent on the actions of the people.

There are Princes of Persia in the spiritual realm working to prevent you from coming into the revelation and reality of your destiny. Something that God wanted to give you twenty-one days ago may be tied up we need to release spiritual warfare and pray: "My God, I ask for the angelic host to resist the enemy's assignments that are keeping back what you promised me in the area of my finances. Now father I ask that they would bring me my answer." Scripture tells us that we don't wrestle against flesh and blood, but demonic powers and principalities.

Ephesians 6:12 For we wrestle not against flesh and blood, but against principalities, against powers, against the rulers of the darkness of this world, against spiritual wickedness in high *places.*

Our spiritual eyes must be open so that we can see what is going on in the heavens. There is not a devil under every bush, but there are more devils under bushes than many Christians are willing to admit. I'm not looking for demons. I don't have to look for them. They are there and I'm aware of them. I know that they want to destroy me but I'm neither afraid of them nor focused on them. I know who I am in Christ.

Know your authority and be vigilant. Even Mary understood this principle regarding prophetic words. After her prophetic word from the angel she responded and prophetically decreed,

Luke 1:38 And Mary said, Behold the handmaid of the Lord; be it unto me according to thy word. And the angel departed from her.

She lined herself up with the Word from heaven, pulled it out of the spiritual realm into existence and birthed it. There's no mistaking it satan has devised a plan of destruction against us. How often have we battled sickness, death, come up short, fought poverty, lack, desolation, or lost sight of our dreams or our divine destiny? However, God has already spoken victory concerning our circumstances. When we make a prophetic decree, we come into agreement with His word. Like earthly, natural kings, who make decrees (sure words that establish things on earth); we too can make decrees which cause things to be done on earth.

Proverbs 8:15 By me kings reign, and princes decree justice. We are called to reign in life as spiritual kings on earth and are instructed to hear and declare His word. As we make declarations of God's Word and will, we will see mighty miracles take place on earth.

Romans 5:17 For if by one man's offence death reigned by one; much more they which receive abundance of grace and of the gift of righteousness shall reign in life by one, Jesus Christ.)

Revelations 5:10 And hast made us unto our God kings and priests: and we shall reign on the earth.

Jeremiah 31:10 Hear the word of the LORD, O ye nations, and declare *it* in the isles afar off, and say, He that scattered Israel will gather him, and keep him, as a shepherd *doth* his flock. Prophetic decrees empower us to release power. Prophetic proclamations unlock and birth our destiny and the revelations, visions and dreams God has given us. The power of God's Word through a prophetic decree will set the captive free, conquer sickness and disease, build and restore God's church and release wealth and prosperity, spiritual and temporal abundance.

We can reverse every decree the enemy has made concerning our lives by issuing a new decree. The devil says you can't, God say you can! The devil says you won't, God say you will! Proclaim what God says about you into the heavens. Take authority over things in the spirit that come against what God has already said about you, call out your miracles and watch your destiny unfold. God gave me revelations that helped birth our entire ministry! Before I entered into ministry, He taught me how we, as Spirit-filled believers, can receive mysteries in the spirit take things out of the invisible through God's creative power and transfer them onto the earthly scene to fulfill our destiny! If you are concerned that it might sound a bit "New Age?" Don't worry. We'll lay out sound biblical principles! (For your reference, what I mean making a prophetic decree is the process of speaking things into existence.)

Revelations 19:11-16 And I saw heaven opened, and behold a white horse; and he that sat upon him *was* called Faithful and True, and in righteousness he doth judge and make war. His eyes *were* as a flame of fire, and on his head *were* many crowns; and he had a name written, that no man knew, but he himself. And he *was* clothed with a vesture dipped in blood: and his name is called The Word of God. And the armies *which were* in heaven followed him upon white horses, clothed in fine linen, white and clean. And out of his mouth goeth a sharp sword, that with it he should smite the nations: and he shall rule them with a rod of iron: and he treadeth the winepress of the fierceness and wrath of Almighty God. And he hath on *his* vesture and on his thigh a name written,

First, I want you to see that the apostle John experienced this revelation when "heaven opened." It's evident that judgment and war happen there. This man, "Faithful and True" used the Word of God to wage this heavenly war: "And out of his mouth goes a sharp sword." Hallelujah. That sharp sword is the rhema word of God, heavenly revelation. In the same way, we must learn how to receive and employ God's Word and God's spoken revelation for our life, to judge and make war in the heavens. We also must learn to resist the forces of darkness that oppose our destiny so that we can bring His words to pass.

Acts 13:2 As they ministered to the Lord, and fasted, the Holy Ghost said, Separate me Barnabas and Saul for the work whereunto I have called them.

Today, if God shows me that He is about to do something, I go home and lay hold of it. It's important to build and plant God's revelation. We need to pray those words through in the spirit and loose them in heaven so they'll be loosed on Earth. The Bible speaks about calling forth those things that are not, as though they already existed. Yes, God is before time, but it's not just about predestination. The Lamb was slain before the foundation of the world. Although everything that God has said in the spiritual realm really exists, He wants us to call forth those things into the tangible, temporal, natural world. However, these things always were and are, in the eternal purpose of God. When I realized these truths, I said, "Wow! Everything I have need of and everything that God wants me to do is in heaven!" It's in heaven now. It's always been in heaven. It's in the eternal purposes of God. We just need to take our divine ATM debit card, insert it into the heavenly realm and punch in the pin number. Hallelujah! Whatever you ask for in prayer, believing, you shall receive it!

Mark 11:24 Therefore I say unto you, What things soever ye desire, when ye pray, believe that ye receive *them,* and ye shall have *them.* We need to make withdrawals from the resources of God to be what God has called us to be. God doesn't just drop it out of the heavenly pie in the sky though. We need to fast and pray for a while. Get out your ATM card, access heaven and make a withdrawal.

Prophetic decrees are used for the sake of the kingdom to destroy works of the enemy or to release life to God's people. However, what we say or decree can also wreak havoc on innocent lives, including our own. They are bitter words spoken in secret about others; or about oneself. They are negative words of gossip, slander, malice or criticism. King David in Psalm 64:1-4 alludes that our mouth is the bow and our words are the arrow. See here what he says about bitter words.

Psalms 64:1-4 To the chief Musician, A Psalm of David. Hear my voice, O God, in my prayer: preserve my life from fear of the enemy. Hide me from the secret counsel of the wicked; from the insurrection of the workers of iniquity: Who whet their tongue like a sword, *and* bend *their bows to shoot* their arrows, *even* bitter words: That they may shoot in secret at the perfect: suddenly do they shoot at him, and fear not. Be careful what you say about people in secret, or behind their backs, because negative words are deadly. They slaughter the innocent, the blameless.

Even words about yourself, like, "I can't do anything right" or, "I'm so stupid" open the doors for the enemy. In fact, the kingdom of darkness enforce negative and bitter words, to destroy lives. It's no wonder Proverbs warns us that death and life are in the power of the tongue.

Proverbs 18:21 Death and life *are* in the power of the tongue: and they that love it shall eat the fruit thereof.

Release arrows of life to bring healing, prosperity and blessing into lives. Say good things about others, declare into the heavens what God says about them. God also wants you to speak out what He has said about you in His word or through prophetic promises to you.

Through prophetic decrees, we can speak things into existence as long as God has already promised those things in Scripture or through a prophetic word. When we receive a word from God, we now have the authority to lay hold of it by faith. We can release arrows of life by speaking about healing. By speaking over our body and speaking over others what the Bible says about miracles, we are activating the power of God's promises we are enforcing things in heaven. Hallelujah! The bow is your mouth. The arrows of the Lord are words. God uses your arrows to deliver you from your foe.

What has God said about you? Proclaim it into the heavens so the devil can hear and tremble. He's trying to keep you from your blessing! Take authority of anything that opposes your calling. What we do or don't do makes or breaks our prophetic word, because everything we have need of originates in heaven. That's where our victory is! When we act, when we loose the Word and God's promises, we bring it to Earth and into our lives, our homes and our ministries. What has God said about your ministry, about your family, your business? Believe these truths and contend for them with your arrows, your words from your mouth.

Dictionaries describe a decree as an authoritative order having the force of law. It's a ruling, an announcement, a declaration, a verdict, a judgment, an order or a pronouncement. It is to decide with authority and usually a legally binding command. Decrees are associated with authority and power.

Decrees in the natural, occur all of the time, especially in government or in courts. In ancient times, most decrees were royal orders, proclaimed publicly by criers (Jonah

3:5-7) or designated "heralds" (Daniel 3:4), often throughout the territory of the monarch (1 Samuel 11:7, Ezra 1:1). Decrees were written and stored in archives for later reference (Ezra 6:1, 2), as in the case of King Cyrus's decree to rebuild God's house. King Darius found the scroll that recorded Cyrus's decree and then issued a decree for advancing the building of God's house. King Cyrus made the original decree and Darius added his own authority and power to back it up for the perfecting of that work (Ezra 6:6-12). The king planned to release the money from his treasury so that the Jews, those returning from captivity, could rebuild the house of God. In effect, the King's message relayed this warning to anyone opposing or challenging his decree, "If anyone tries to alter this decree... remember that I am King. My word carries weight!

Whoever alters this decree shall be hung on the rafter of his house. Let his house be as a refuse heap and a dunghill. Let that happen to anyone who attempts to come against this decree. In ancient times, people would never defy the decree of a king because they would pay for their disobedience with their lives. Even today, there are consequences for breaking that which is decreed to be the law of the land.

Now, if natural decrees are that powerful, how much more powerful are spiritual decrees? Scripture calls New Testament believers "priests and kings" of the Most High God (1 Peter 2:5; Revelations 1:4-6). In many societies, there is no higher calling than to be a priest or king. Yet that is what God has called each of us as believers to be. "You also, as livings stones, are being built up a spiritual house, a holy priesthood, to offer up spiritual sacrifices acceptable to God through Jesus Christ" (1 Peter 2:5). We are as a kingdom of priests with Christ as High Priest and King of Kings over all.

In Israel, priests and kings were divinely appointed, appointed by God, not elected or self-appointed. After being chosen, God delegated them with authority, with the power to act on His behalf for the good of the people. As believers, divinely appointed priests and kings of God's Kingdom, delegated with His authority, what do you think happens when we actually decree into the spiritual realm and make known the manifold wisdom of God to demonic powers and principalities? The enemy cannot invade our house. The angelic hosts of heaven and Jesus Himself will backup our decrees those that line up with His scriptural or revelatory words to us. You have been given kingly anointing and authority; you've been made to sit in heavenly places (Ephesians 2:6). Every demon in hell trembles at your words when you know your position in Christ! They know that behind everything you say is the authority of heaven and Jesus Christ. The angels of God will come and arrest them. God releases angels to carry out His word in your life when you release the Word in heaven.

This is spiritual warfare. The enemy knows if you're unsure of your authority. If you are uncertain of whom you are in Christ and then get sure! Ask God for a revelation of which you are in Christ and receive that certainty that He, the hope of glory, lives in you. Here are some scripture verses to boost your confidence: John 1:12; 15:15; Romans 5:1; 8:28; 8:31-39; 1 Corinthians 6:17; Ephesians 1:3-8; Ephesians 2:10; 3:12; Colossians1:13, 14 2:9, 10; Hebrews 4:14-16; Philippians 4:3.

Are you ready to release a few arrows into the heavenly realm? If you've seen the movie,

Brave Heart, you may remember a scene where the archers gathered, waited and then suddenly released their arrows at the same time. Those fiery arrows lit up the whole sky! That's what happens in the heavens as you make decrees.

It's time to decree what God has promised you and what He has said about you. It's time to declare what the Bible and the prophetic words have said about you. You are going to make powerful prayers of proclamation of decree! Isaiah 55:11 So shall my word be that goeth forth out of my mouth: it shall not return unto me void, but it shall accomplish that which I please, and it shall prosper *in the thing* whereto I sent it. Start by reminding the devil about your destiny words from God. Speak all those prophetic words, visions and revelations God has given you. Place a whole quiver of arrows (God's promises) on your back. Ready? Did God promise prosperity? Take your arrow, place it in your bow and release it! Say, "Spirit of poverty, God has said I would prosper, 'Beloved, I wish above all that thou mayest prosper and be in health, even as thy soul prospereth' (3 John 1:2, KJV). His word is true and you will not hinder me."

These are your words that you speak with priestly or kingly authority and the King of King's word backs you up! "My God, you promised me healing and prosperity. You listen to me devil of poverty, devil of sickness you will not prevail!" Shoot! Shoot! Prophesy! Prophesy! Take out another arrow; load it in your bow, aim toward the heavens and let that hindering devil know you are taking authority! "God's will is "good, pleasing and perfect"! (Romans 12:2). Release God's promises in your life for revival, miracles, health and salvation for loved ones. Release arrows against opposing forces. Shoot against religiosity! Shoot against unbelief! Shoot against apathy! "Father, I release revival!" Keep shooting! Keep going the heavens are opening. Grab another arrow out of your quiver, "Father, I want miracles! You promised miracles. Line up your sights; take aim, shoot and say "Be healed in Jesus' name!" Then take authority against demons of infirmity, devils of sickness, every demon of disease.

Keep going! Don't stop! The weapons of our warfare are mighty through God! Take out an arrow for your family and say, "God, I want my household saved! I want my entire household saved, Jesus! I take aim against the God of this world that has blinded their hearts and minds. Father, I release and prophesy the arrow of the glorious Gospel of Truth, that it may pierce the hearts of those in my house." Now, for every person in your house you want saved, call them by name and tell them to come out of darkness. Proclaim liberty to the captives. Hallelujah! You are making known to demonic powers and principalities in the heavens your knowledge of the manifold wisdom of God.

Many fail to understand and apply the principle of spiritual aggression as they contend for their destiny. We see this principle in Matthew 11:12; "And from the days of John the Baptist until now the kingdom of heaven suffers violence, and the violent take it by force." The context of the Greek word used for violent in this passage isn't the same usage we apply it to today, in the natural.

Most violence today lands us in trouble! Rather, it describes a believer who is aggressive, zealous and energetic in taking what has been made available to him or her. In this passage also, we are invited to seize the Kingdom of God! This means that the Kingdom isn't just going to "fall in our laps."

We have to covet, then take or seize, or lay hold of the Kingdom. The apostle Paul told the Corinthians to "covet earnestly the best gifts." Covet your promises and what God has said about you! People pressed into touch the hem of Jesus' garments. They cried out in loud voices until He stopped by. They tore roofs off houses to get healing for a loved one. Shoot those arrows; take the Kingdom of heaven by force! Be aggressive, be relentless.

God won't reprove you for raising the roof! He won't admonish you for your intensity! Aim and shoot those arrows of life. There's no limit on signs, wonders and miracles! Just press in and lay hold of them. Be earnest, be zealous. Never by satisfied, Birth your destiny. Your decrees carry weight to activate all of God's promises.

Living a Life of Victory

I want you to know that we can live a life of victory daily. This chapter is sure to inspire you. In this timely message, I'll examine the power and limitations brought about by our words, thoughts, affiliations, giving and favor. We received God's gentle and uplifting approach to these five key aspects of spiritual growth will lead you to a deeper relationship with our Lord. You will discover how God wants you to prosper physically, financially, emotionally and spiritually as a testimony to His great power and love.

Expect signs and wonders, in the form of healings and breakthroughs, as you worship God and implement these valuable principles into your walk with Christ.

Mark 10:29, 30 And Jesus answered and said, Verily I say unto you, There is no man that hath left house, or brethren, or sisters, or father, or mother, or wife, or children, or lands, for my sake, and the gospel's, But he shall receive an hundredfold now in this time, houses, and brethren, and sisters, and mothers, and children, and lands, with persecutions; and in the world to come eternal life. I firmly believe that God wants us to prosper in all things and be in good health, just as our soul prospers, exactly as,

3 John 1:2 Beloved, I wish above all things that thou mayest prosper and be in health, even as thy soul prospereth. His desire is to possess you, empower you and prosper you. In fact, everything He does for you and in your life is for your good.

As you trust and follow Him, you will see God's faithfulness to you as He blesses your life with good things.

Psalms 84:11 For the LORD God *is* a sun and shield: the LORD will give grace and glory: no good *thing* will he withhold from them that walk uprightly. I will share keys that will help you unlock some doors in your life.

You will eat the fruit of your mouth Galatians 6:7 Be not deceived; God is not mocked: for whatsoever a man soweth, that shall he also reap.

Jeremiah 1:12 Then said the LORD unto me, Thou hast well seen: for I will hasten my word to perform it. God is He who raises the dead, brings into existence and removes from existence, controls all creation and is the Creator of all things in heaven, earth and below the earth. God spoke all things into existence with His word.

Because man is created in His image, we, too have the ability to speak things into existence. That's why we must sow good seeds by speaking good words. To be blessed in our own lives, we must sow words of blessings over our nation, our children, our neighbors, our fellow brothers and sisters in Christ.

Job 22:28 Thou shalt also decree a thing, and it shall be established unto thee: and the light shall shine upon thy ways. We must believe and profess words of life over all things because God is always listening and He desires to bless, enrich and empower His children according to the words they speak. So it is important to decree the blessing over yourself, over your circumstances, over your finances and over your family according to the word of God. You will see it come to pass in your life. If you decree "blessing" several times a day, it will become a habit and the results will be tremendous.

So, in order to experience God's full blessing, we need to have a deep hunger and desire to see change come to pass in our lives. As well, we need to be fully prepared to focus on that change. I have heard it said, "Doing the same thing over and over again and expecting different results is the definition of insanity."

Numbers 14:28 Say unto them, *As truly as* I live, saith the LORD, as ye have spoken in mine ears, so will I do to you: Negative Conversation: Speaking words of negativity limits what God can do

Proverbs 18:21 Death and life *are* in the power of the tongue: and they that love it shall eat the fruit thereof.

Ephesians 4:29 Let no corrupt communication proceed out of your mouth, but that which is good to the use of edifying, that it may minister grace unto the hearers.

When we speak negative words, we are agreeing with the enemy whom the Bible says is the father of lies. For example, if a Gardner doesn't pull the weeds in a flower bed, the flowers won't flourish and remain beautiful. Their life will be choked out! Just the same, there are things in our own lives that we must remove in order for us to grow. To guarantee maturity and a winning life, you must eliminate all of the weeds of negativity from your life. When we speak God's word, His power is present to perform His word in our lives.

We are all called to work from the resting place of God, a state without any striving. This is done by setting our eyes on the Lord the Author and Perfecter of our faith, ruling and reigning from that place of rest where we are seated with Christ in heavenly places. So keep God in your thoughts at all times. By continuously centering your thoughts on God and scriptural truth, wrong thinking will be crowded out, you'll be empowered during temptation, and you'll develop wisdom for important decisions. Equally, you need to meditate on God's word; this is the daily bread for your life that will cause you to thrive. In the book of Luke, Jesus overcame the enemy who tempted Him in the wilderness by knowing the word of God; likewise, it is important to know who you are in Christ and who He is in you. For those who may struggle in this area, I suggest finding a meeting place, an upper room in your house where you can encounter God daily.

Hosea 4:6 My people are destroyed for lack of knowledge: because thou hast rejected knowledge, I will also reject thee, that thou shalt be no priest to me: seeing thou hast forgotten the law of thy God, I will also forget thy children.

I would suggest a good start would be with three chapters a day in your Bible. After all, knowledge and faith go hand in hand. There are times I have felt that I do not have enough faith. This is when I turn to my Bible and begin to read out loud. As I am calling out His promises, I suddenly feel strengthened and ready to preach the gospel to bring hope to the hopeless. Faith is released when you know what the word says about you.

Romans 8:26, 27 Likewise the Spirit also helpeth our infirmities: for we know not what we should pray for as we ought: but the Spirit itself maketh intercession for us with groanings which cannot be uttered. And he that searcheth the hearts knoweth what *is* the mind of the Spirit, because he maketh intercession for the saints according to *the will of* God.

So, a way of being conscious of God is to pray in tongues, the heavenly language of God, as often as we can. We can do this while driving, typing an e-mail, doing dished or even walking. Why should we choose to pray this way? Because this is when the Holy Spirit prays the right kind of prayer through us with groaning and words that we, ourselves, cannot utter.

Daily lifting Jesus higher in our lives is another way we can be God-conscious. We achieve this by praising and worshiping Him as our Creator and Source and being thankful to our Maker, who is in control of all things. He likes to hear our praise and worship and it blesses His heart no matter how it sounds! By pulling the heavenly realm down through worship, two great benefits come to pass we're rejuvenated and the atmosphere around us changes. Even medical doctors witness the difference between those sick patients who praise and worship and those who don't praise and worship shifts things in the spirit realm. It acts like a key that unlocks some of the doors in our lives.

Just look at what happened to Paul and Silas when they were imprisoned. As Hopelessness permeated the atmosphere around them, they began to sing praises to God and to pull the glory down from heaven. As a result, by divine intervention, they were released from their chains and this supernatural feat caused the jailer and his household to be saved. No wonder it is wise to have praise and worship music flowing throughout our homes all the time! This keeps the atmosphere clean and sends evil away. I believe as the praises go up, so does God's delight in us; and then His blessings come down in return. You can never out-give God!

Proverbs 13:20 He that walketh with wise *men* shall be wise: but a companion of fools shall be destroyed.

This world is noted for its self-sufficiency, yet thousands of people are suffering because they don't have the right mentors in their lives. "You show me your friends and I'll tell you your future." Use wisdom and be selective in choosing your friendships those whom you associate with as well as the voices that "feed" you. Friends will add or take away from your life. Why? Because, wrong relationships will confuse both your mind and your spirit. When building relationships, ask yourself: "Will this friendship bring me closer to Jesus? Or will it soil the beauty of what God has begun?" Stay away from anything that will bring you down. Do no entangle yourself nor continue to stay in relationships that are stagnant or pulling you downhill. When no one is around, good books make good mentors. I read books by men and women such as Smith Wigglesworth, Kathryn Kuhlman, to name just a couple.

God doesn't want us to be confused by wrong thoughts or relationships; His desire is for us to flourish in all that He has to offer. Likewise, in point four of this teaching, we discover how God promises to respond to our giving. In fact, He invites us to expect great things when we live in Him. In my next point, we will learn how God wants us to live a full life in his favor. Giving is a characteristic of God.

John 3:16 For God so loved the world, that he gave his only begotten Son, that whosoever believeth in him should not perish, but have everlasting life.

God promises to respond to our giving.

Luke 6:38 Give, and it shall be given unto you; good measure, pressed down, and shaken together, and running over, shall men give into your bosom. For with the same measure that ye mete withal it shall be measured to you again.

Malachi 3:10, 11 Bring ye all the tithes into the storehouse, that there may be meat in mine house, and prove me now herewith, saith the LORD of hosts, if I will not open you the windows of heaven, and pour you out a blessing, that *there shall* not *be room* enough *to receive it.* And I will rebuke the devourer for your sakes, and he shall not destroy the fruits of your ground; neither shall your vine cast her fruit before the time in the field, saith the LORD of hosts.

God always reacts in faith. Jesus marveled at faith. It impresses all of heaven! Sow with great expectation. God treasures the giver. He sees His own nature in you and honors it with the promise of prosperity. God is attracted to us when we sow in expectation because there is power in expectation. Now is the time for believers to do what they have never done in order to get what they never had. Sow bountifully to receive bountifully.

Like a wise farmer, we really need to know the seasons we are in according to God's calendar.

Ecclesiastes 3:1 To every *thing there is* a season, and a time to every purpose under the heaven:

When you release what is in your hand, God will release back what is in His hand. Seeds need to be planted in the right season to reap the blessing of God in the proper season. Another type of sowing and reaping is the gift of hospitality; sowing into peoples lives by taking care of men and women of God.

2 Kings 4:8-17 And it fell on a day, that Elisha passed to Shunem, where *was* a great woman; and she constrained him to eat bread. And *so* it was, *that* as oft as he passed by, he turned in thither to eat bread. And she said unto her husband, Behold now, I perceive that this *is* an holy man of God, which passeth by us continually. Let us make a little chamber, I pray thee, on the wall; and let us set for him there a bed, and a table, and a stool, and a candlestick: and it shall be, when he cometh to us, that he shall turn in thither. And it fell on a day, that he came thither, and he turned into

the chamber, and lay there. And he said to Gehazi his servant, Call this Shunammite. And when he had called her, she stood before him. And he said unto him, Say now unto her, Behold, thou hast been careful for us with all this care; what *is* to be done for thee? wouldest thou be spoken for to the king, or to the captain of the host? And she answered, I dwell among mine own people. And he said, What then *is* to be done for her? And Gehazi answered, Verily she hath no child, and her husband is old. And he said, Call her. And when he had called her, she stood in the door. And he said, About this season, according to the time of life, thou shalt embrace a son. And she said, Nay, my lord, *thou* man of God, do not lie unto thine handmaid. And the woman conceived, and bare a son at that season that Elisha had said unto her, according to the time of life. We see in the above scripture that, Elisha had stayed with a Shunammite woman and her husband many times.

The woman had taken time to cook for and serve Elisha and Gehazi, his servant. One day she said to her husband that she wanted to make a room for this man of God and flourish it so that each time he was in the area he would have a place to rest. Because of their hospitality, Elisha felt it was important to bless them in return and in talking with the servant, Elisha found out that she was barren. Then he said, "About this time next year you shall embrace a son" And she did! Then, after being impressed by the Shunammite woman's story and upon the leading of the Holy Spirit, as we were leaving we asked the couple if there were any pressing needs in their lives. They told us that since they were still childless after seventeen years of marriage, they were praying for a child. Believing that God would grant them that request, we prayed with them. Just recently, we found out that a baby was finally conceived. Glory to Jesus!

This couple had made room for us in their home, they honored the servants of God by giving of their time and material possessions and in return God honored them with the gift of their baby, the desire of their hearts.

The next chapter is on favor but I want to end this chapter by talking a little about it here. One day of favor is worth a lifetime of labor. Here are four truths about what favor is. One, favor is the divine way; not the substitute. Two, favor is an attitude of goodness towards you, not an exchange of payment for something you have done. Three, favor is the secret hidden and unspoken dream of every human living today and can turn tragedy into triumph within moments.

Four, you cannot work hard enough or long enough to get everything you deserve and to be debt-free. Actually, the sum total of these four truths has affected me to the point that I believe we are in a season for pressing in for financial blessing and financial breakthrough. As well, I believe that we are in a season of great soul harvest and therefore, God wants to prosper us, fill us and make us debt free so we can do kingdom work. Our Lord said that He has come to give us a life of fullness! When God's favor comes into your life, a "nobody" becomes "a somebody." An example of this is found in the story of Esther.

Esther 2:16 So Esther was taken unto king Ahasuerus into his house royal in the tenth month, which *is* the month Tebeth, in the seventh year of his reign. I believe that God is not a "respecter of persons" and what He has done for these precious ones He can do for you.

When we remember the words spoken in,

Romans 8:31-37 What shall we then say to these things? If God *be* for us, who *can be* against us? He that spared not his own Son, but delivered him up for us all, how shall he not with him also freely give us all things? Who shall lay any thing to the charge of God's elect? *It is* God that justifieth. Who *is* he that condemneth? *It is* Christ that died, yea rather, that is risen again, who is even at the right hand of God, who also maketh intercession for us. Who shall separate us from the love of Christ? *Shall* tribulation, or distress, or persecution, or famine, or nakedness, or peril, or sword? As it is written, For thy sake we are killed all the day long; we are accounted as sheep for the slaughter. Nay, in all these things we are more than conquerors through him that loved us. Just like an athlete who prepares himself for a race, we, too, need to prepare ourselves for the spiritual race... "To run the race this is set before us."

So my encouragement for you is this: Expect from Him who is able to do more than you could think or imagine according to His great power. As you meditate upon these keys, here is my prayer for you: "Lord, I thank you for your goodness and faithfulness and the great blessings that follow us because of our obedience to your word. Thank you for these testimonies. I pray that those reading this message will be greatly encouraged to apply these five keys in their lives and that they will experience great blessings as a result. Lord, may they prosper in all that they do, physically, financially and spiritually. Touch them by the power of your word and make them a blessing for others. In Jesus' name. AMEN."

Supernatural Favor

God is looking to show His goodness and favor on His chosen ones. The day of Manifestation Impartation of Favor is a dynamic chapter that will encourage and strengthen you to run your race of destiny triumphantly! I'll share prophetically about the hour of increased favor that is coming upon faithful believers today, favor that empowers and favor that releases greater authority, grace, spiritual blessings and supernatural provision for harvest. You will discover what delights the Lord and how to position yourself before God so that the dew of heaven, the anointing of favor and an overcoming spirit crowns your life. Get ready to birth great fruit! We live in the most exciting age of all time. We are closer now to experiencing the greatest spiritual harvest since Pentecost. This is the hour of God's favor. It is the season of holy commissioning, destiny, empowering and sending the day of a mighty move of the Holy Spirit without measure. The dew of the Lord is coming down and when it lifts there will be manna lots of it. God is releasing showers of blessing on His chosen saints. The former rain and latter rain have converged for the harvest. The dew of heaven is resting on the seeds that have been on your heart, the seeds of destiny that have fallen upon dry ground. The dew the latter rain and the spring rain are coming. The seeds are budding and soon they will yield much fruit.

Many have walked faithfully in the Spirit but haven't come into the day of increase, favor and authority. But this day is coming, as it did for Jesus and many great biblical saints. Scripture says that Jesus increased and kept increasing in wisdom and stature and in favor with God and men.

Luke 2:52 And Jesus increased in wisdom and stature, and in favour with God and man.

John the Baptist, the son of Zechariah and Elizabeth grew in wisdom, knowledge and fortitude in his soul and was in the deserts,

Luke 1:80 And the child grew, and waxed strong in spirit, and was in the deserts till the day of his shewing unto Israel.

God's favor increased over King David. The Spirit of God came upon David when he was appointed king over Israel, but it took years before his kingship manifested; where he actually ruled and reigned over all of Israel. David received more measures of favor and authority when he reigned as king and even more as he grew as king. Every stage of his faithful, intimate walk with the Lord manifested more favor.

1 Samuel 16:1-13 And the LORD said unto Samuel, How long wilt thou mourn for Saul, seeing I have rejected him from reigning over Israel? fill thine horn with oil, and go, I will send thee to Jesse the Bethlehemite: for I have provided me a king among his sons. And Samuel said, How can I go? If Saul hear *it,* he will kill me. And the LORD said, Take an heifer with thee, and say, I am come to sacrifice to the LORD. And call Jesse to the sacrifice, and I will shew thee what thou shalt do: and thou shalt anoint unto me *him* whom I name unto thee. And Samuel did that which the LORD spake, and came to Bethlehem. And the elders of the town trembled at his coming, and said, Comest thou peaceably? And he said, Peaceably: I am come to sacrifice unto the LORD: sanctify yourselves,

and come with me to the sacrifice. And he sanctified Jesse and his sons, and called them to the sacrifice. And it came to pass, when they were come, that he looked on Eliab, and said, Surely the LORD'S anointed *is* before him. But the LORD said unto Samuel, Look not on his countenance, or on the height of his stature; because I have refused him: for *the LORD seeth* not as man seeth; for man looketh on the outward appearance, but the LORD looketh on the heart. Then Jesse called Abinadab, and made him pass before Samuel. And he said, Neither hath the LORD chosen this. Then Jesse made Shammah to pass by. And he said, Neither hath the LORD chosen this. Again, Jesse made seven of his sons to pass before Samuel. And Samuel said unto Jesse, The LORD hath not chosen these. And Samuel said unto Jesse, Are here all *thy* children? And he said, There remaineth yet the youngest, and, behold, he keepeth the sheep. And Samuel said unto Jesse, Send and fetch him: for we will not sit down till he come hither. And he sent, and brought him in. Now he *was* ruddy, *and* withal of a beautiful countenance, and goodly to look to. And the LORD said, Arise, anoint him: for this *is* he. Then Samuel took the horn of oil, and anointed him in the midst of his brethren: and the Spirit of the LORD came upon David from that day forward. So Samuel rose up, and went to Ramah. The fullness of the Spirit of God comes upon us when we accept Jesus into our hearts and He gives us that initial measure of gifts and Holy Spirit power. However, these measures of gifts and blessings also increase as we seek to increase in favor with God.

The Spirit of the Lord says that God is placing a crown of manifestation on the heads of His faithful, diligent, chosen saints a crown of great favor and authority with God and men a new and greater installment of the fruits and blessings of the Spirit. A measure comes; another measure, another and another. God rewards those who diligently seek Him.

Hebrews 11:6 But without faith *it is* impossible to please *him:* for he that cometh to God must believe that he is, and *that* he is a rewarder of them that diligently seek him. To those He calls His friends are greater measures of authority and favor.

Favor is God's "pleasure." When God takes pleasure or delights in people, He distinguishes and delights in them, showering down His spiritual blessing, goodwill and grace. He wants to bestow on us His unsearchable riches that enrich us with all spiritual blessings, in faith and with the riches of grace and of glory, with no sorrow accompanying them. We have entered into a time of increased favor, when God will empower and commission believers for harvest with greater authority, grace, spiritual blessing, faith and supernatural provision. It is a season of birth a season when His saints step into the fullness of His grace and birth great fruit, a season when God births and releases ministries and destinies.

The fruit we bear glorifies God and He says that He will anoint His diligent saints with an even greater manifestation of spiritual riches! He will favor the faithful with His riches.

Proverbs 10:22 The blessing of the LORD, it maketh rich, and he addeth no sorrow with it. He will literally pour His blessings upon the hands of the diligent.

Proverbs 10:4 He becometh poor that dealeth *with* a slack hand: but the hand of the diligent maketh rich.

They will receive a new installment, an anointing of incredible depths of spiritual riches. His favor will cause them success. They will be the head and not the tail because of the favor He will pour over them... Experience won't be necessary because they'll have His favor, which empowers and therefore qualifies them to accomplish great feats. God is commissioning His saints upon whom His favor rests, with grace to do the impossible. God's glory will fall upon those in whom God delights.

Moses placed Aaron's rod before the ark and it miraculously blossomed and bore almonds a symbol of God's favor in choosing Aaron as high priest. In the culture of the Israelites, the rod symbolized authority. It was a tool used by the shepherd to correct and guide his flock.

Psalms 23:4 Yea, though I walk through the valley of the shadow of death, I will fear no evil: for thou *art* with me; thy rod and thy staff they comfort me.

Both Aaron and Moses' rods were symbols of authority and endowed with miraculous power. With Moses' rod, God parted the Red Sea and brought forth water from a stone. God used

Aaron's rod in His dealings with stubborn Pharaoh. This is the season of choosing. God is placing the rod of kingship, favor and authority in the hand of the chosen and it's going to bud man, it's going to blossom, it's going to bear fruit! God wants to favor you. Consider Esther He gave her everything she needed to receive the favor He desired for her. God gave her favor with Hegai who provided what she needed and advanced her to the best place in the king's harem (Esther 2). This was a supernatural provision of grace.

Years ago in an encounter, the Holy Spirit spoke to me and told me that I was one of many "first fruits sons and daughters" that would birth a ministry in a day. It was that quick. God's favor was upon me; because I sought Him with all of my heart I pursued Him and prepared myself to be chosen. So too, the Lord is choosing, giving authority, power and favor with men. Doors will swing open as God supernaturally provides in this day of manifestation. But the Lord says, that you must have the grace to receive His favor, "There's a see time and there is a harvest time. There is a time to sow and a time to reap. There's a time to labor in intercession, as Elijah did and then there's manifestation!"

There are seasons in which God ordains seed time and seasons where God ordains harvest. There are times to throw your bread upon the water and times it multiplies back to you. This is the season of multiplication, of manifestation, of God giving you what you desire. Even if you've asked a hundred times for one thing, in the season of favor, the heavens open and He grants what you ask of Him. Esther prepared and positioned herself to be pleasing before the king. So pleased was he, that he held out a golden scepter to her, signifying his favor and an invitation into the palace. The king asked her, "What do you wish?" This is the day that God selects those pleasing to Him and asks, "What do you wish?"

Favor depends on friendship. Through intimacy, the Lord calls us His "friend".

John 15:15 Henceforth I call you not servants; for the servant knoweth not what his lord doeth: but I have called you friends; for all things that I have heard of my Father I have made known unto you. In friendship with Him, we are no longer servants. When we abide in Him we can ask anything we desire and it shall be granted to us.

John 15:7 If ye abide in me, and my words abide in you, ye shall ask what ye will, and it shall be done unto you. Favor depends on preparing ourselves and positioning ourselves to be pleasing before the King. It's time in the tabernacle, in the tent of meeting, meeting with God, worshiping and spending intimate time with Him. It moves God when we prepare and delights Him to respond to our desires. Hosts of angels await the Lord's command in heaven to release and manifest His blessings.

God bestowed a great deal of honor upon Aaron, anointing him high priest and providing him with abundance, authority and blessings, all by reason of favor! Because of His favor, you will receive a holy commissioning, backed by heaven, backed by God and the fullness of your calling and breakthrough will manifest.

You will become a man or woman approved by God with His seal, His evidence and His witness upon you. The gifts and the power manifesting through you will bear the witness of God.

Acts 2:22 Ye men of Israel, hear these words; Jesus of Nazareth, a man approved of God among you by miracles and wonders and signs, which God did by him in the midst of you, as ye yourselves also know: Jesus Himself often traced His power to do great things to His commission from the Father and He did it in such a way as to show He was closely united to Him.

John 5:19 Then answered Jesus and said unto them, Verily, verily, I say unto you, The Son can do nothing of himself, but what he seeth the Father do: for what things soever he doeth, these also doeth the Son likewise.

John 5:30 I can of mine own self do nothing: as I hear, I judge: and my judgment is just; because I seek not mine own will, but the will of the Father which hath sent me.

Peter says that God did these works by Jesus Christ, to show that Jesus was truly sent by Him and that therefore He had the seal and signs of God's approval. Jesus Himself said in John,

John 5:36 But I have greater witness than *that* of John: for the works which the Father hath given me to finish, the same works that I do, bear witness of me, that the Father hath sent me. The evidence of favor will be on everything you touch. The rod will produce. It will bring forth.

Acts 4:33, 34 And with great power gave the apostles witness of the resurrection of the Lord Jesus: and great grace was upon them all. Neither was there any among them that lacked: for as many as were possessors of lands or houses sold them, and brought the prices of the things that were sold,

Many Christians have lacked the favor of God. Favor does away with lack! Those with the rod will not lack! Great power brought great favor and favor brought provision because of great grace because there was a great witness. They gave witness with great power to the resurrection of the Lord Jesus. Because of favor, the apostles didn't have to preach about the resurrection or proclaim it; they gave witness to it, proof, a demonstration of their divine authority to heal the sick and cast out demons. This is where the church is headed, to that place of giving witness a demonstration, manifestation, proof, evidence and testimony of personal experience and of victory. God is going to prove and back up your calling. He's going to place the rod in your hand and you will have the right and the authority to use it. Before you had the power, but you didn't have the "right." You will now have influence, a platform and doors will open you never dreamed possible.

You are called, just as the disciples were, but Jesus selected twelve to send out with authority over sickness and demons.

Matthew 10:1 And when he had called unto *him* his twelve disciples, he gave them power *against* unclean spirits, to cast them out, and to heal all manner of sickness and all manner of disease.

Moses waited years in the desert for the day of manifestation. He had the promise. He had friendship. He had favor. Even though his call existed before the foundation of the world, just as ours does, it wasn't time for commissioning until God gave him the rod, the right and the privilege to advance. The rod represented influence, authority and divine backup; witness from God that He sent you, a witness that no man can deny.

Many are called but few are chosen. There is a calling. God is choosing. He's going to bestow an impartation of authority and favor.

You'll have the "right" to use dunamis power. Things will accelerate. Doors will open. The blessings of the Lord will multiply. Your destiny, visions, dreams will birth. The latter rain and former rain will converge for harvest. I call forth the seed and the promise that's already here. Let the dew of heaven fall upon you. Favor is coming. With the impartation of authority, chains and shackles will fall off. You'll break free of tethers. The anointing will break the yoke. You shall make decrees that set the captives free, to proclaim liberty for those who are oppressed. God will give you what you desire. You will plunder the Egyptians and experience spiritual breakthrough. You will have the spirit of an over comer, a victorious, triumphant spirit. The tide will change and release the spirit of the overcomer. God will fill up the holes of lack, for the blessings of the Lord maketh one rich.

The rod of the one whom God chooses will blossom, as our ways please Him, He will increase His favor, measure by measure. This is the season of manifestation of His favor. Will you wear the crown of manifestation? Will you advance into the tent of witness? Position yourself for the dew of the Lord the anointing of favor. Pursue intimate friendship with the

Lord. Let yours be the rod that blooms and then expect an open heaven over your life as His glory comes down and manifests His supernatural, astonishing blessings on your life. Let the almonds come forth!

Financial Breakthrough

It has been a season of Christians losing ground, especially in the financial realm. God spoke to my heart about breakthrough. Here we go let's start off with a prayer. In the name of Jesus of Nazareth, I bind and break all principalities and powers, thrones, dominions and strongmen off your family, friends, church family and yourself. I bind and break off Baal the false god in Jesus Name. I also bind and forbid the false god Baal from influencing your family, friends, church family and yourself in Jesus Name. I bind and break the false god of wealth from keeping its hold on America in Jesus Name. I bind and break the spirit of mammon unrighteousness and bitterness from operating in your family, friends, church family and myself in Jesus Name. I bind and break the false god of money from mind control and releasing fear upon your family, friends, church family and yourself in Jesus Name. I bind and break money from having power over the thoughts, will and emotions. I bind and break worry and anxiety over money in Jesus name. I bind and break the mindsets of; never having enough, I can't afford it, impulse buying, stinginess, greed, discontentment, bondage to debt and exaggerated importance of money in Jesus Name. I bind and break all the symptoms of the spirit of mammon in Jesus Name.

Matthew 6:24 "No man can serve two masters: for either he will hate the one and love the other; or else he will hold to the one and despise the other. Ye cannot serve God and mammon."

God is your source and you will not have to fear for what you need. God is Jehovah Jirah your provider.

Philippians 4:19 "But my God shall supply all your need according to his riches in glory by Christ Jesus."

Matthew 6:31 "Therefore take no thought, saying, what shall we eat? Or, what shall we drink? Or, Wherewithal shall we be clothed?"

I bind and break any and all transference of spirits. I bind and break greed, covertness and the ability to use people to get money in Jesus Name. I bind and break in the Name of Jesus the spirit of depression. I bind and break depression from rising up where money is concerned in my family, friends, church family and yourself in Jesus Name. I bind and break the love of money in Jesus Name. The wealth of the wicked is laid up for the righteous in Jesus Name.

Pray:
Lord Jesus, cause me to be a faithful servant to sow seeds, offerings and a giving tithe to the local church. Make me Lord Jesus, a manager of money for Kingdom purpose. Lord Jesus cause my mind will and emotions to know money is to serve me for Kingdom purpose. (Not for me to serve money.) Lord Jesus stir up my faith where giving is concerned. Lord Jesus make me accountable with my finances. Open my ears to hear the voice of the Lord and my eyes to see in the Holy Spirit. Release the Spirit of wisdom for finances in Jesus Name. Amen.

Dreams of God

I learned after years of having dreams not being fulfilled, that I could dream with God. This will change your life if you take hold of it. When we open ourselves to dream of doing things bigger than we can do ourselves, if the vision is rooted in the Word of God, if it has the heart of Christ, and if it will give God and God alone the glory, God will come on the scene. Now, more than ever before, we the people of God individually and corporately as the Body of Christ, need to have such vision for lost souls, a vision that stretches beyond our own limitations, beyond what we can do ourselves, because we need God's presence big time. Where there is no vision, souls are lost. Where there is no vision, people really do perish.

Just as salvation is a heart matter, visions are matters of the heart, too because they are a reflection or pictures of Christ's heart and of what we believe and how much we believe for.

The Bible teaches,
Philippians 2:3-5 *Let* nothing *be done* through strife or vainglory; but in lowliness of mind let each esteem other better than themselves. Look not every man on his own things, but every man also on the things of others. Let this mind be in you, which was also in Christ Jesus:

Next to salvation, visions are likely one of the most vital aspects of our faith for this very reason. Do we have the heart of Christ for the lost? Do we believe big enough and beyond ourselves and beyond our own ability? Is our vision, both individual and collective is it big enough, desperate enough and beyond us for God to show up in His power? Having vision is to have a future direction.

Good News! Without a doubt, God gives priority to the future over the past! What happened in the past might be important but the future is of the greatest importance to God. That ultimate future that He has planned is greater than we are, more awesome than we can imagine and involves the completion of what He originally intended for His creation. God knows what the future looks like, to be sure if we open ourselves to God-sized dreams, we will experience something new and far beyond our own expectations. Furthermore, trust that God gives us a vision for something; He will always provide what we need to accomplish it.

God is challenging us and asking, "Who do you say I am? Am I the supernatural God able to do more than you can imagine, intervening today in unique supernatural ways that are way beyond your understanding or ability, or not?"

We can't duck and hide for cover any longer, we owe Him an answer. God's high purpose involves gathering, by His Spirit, a faithful, radical remnant of believers; brings them into a "culture" where creed, race, rank and age all melt away, where a heart for lost souls and revival for harvest is the high mark, the standard and the norm. A culture where God's people understand the times and prepare their hearts to believe beyond the past and toward the ultimate plan of the greater good, the greater works, the greater glory.

There has never before been a more important hour in the history of the church than now for a vision for the souls that are still lost. Whether it is an individual crying out for help, a family, a city, or a nation, we need to see what Paul saw in a vision in the night and hear what he heard through the man from Macedonia: "The cry of lost humanity, of hurting hearts, of the captives, of the man saying, Come, help us!"

Then we need to follow the vision, as Paul followed it to Philippi in Macedonia, in one of the most profound, dramatic revivals the world had ever seen. According to Acts chapter 16, the earth shook, jails were destroyed, shackles loosed, cities stirred, people were saved, whole families were baptized and the works and miracles of God went on and on and on from the midnight hours into the dawn into the days into the cities as the lost heard and responded to the Gospel Truth. Can you imagine or believe for such a revival in your family let alone your city?

Following my dramatic change a few years ago, for months I spent for the most part saturated in His word and in His presence, I constantly dreamed about preaching, being a vessel of God to bring healing to my family and to the multitudes. From early on in my walk with God, having emptied my heart of myself, I opened my heart and life wide for the heart and purposes of Christ Jesus and He gave me a passionate heart for the lost. God's dreams for us are always bigger than our own. While I prayed for multitudes, God had greater plans! Can you imagine? Oh, this still excites me. One day, while meditating on the goodness of God and hungering for my dream to see souls saved, miracles and more the Holy Spirit impressed upon me a verse from.

Psalms 2:8 Ask of me, and I shall give *thee* the heathen *for* thine inheritance, and the uttermost parts of the earth *for* thy possession. Wow! Nations! At that moment, God captured my heart for a million lost souls won for Him. A million!

Deuteronomy 8:18 But thou shalt remember the LORD thy God: for *it is* he that giveth thee power to get wealth, that he may establish his covenant which he sware unto thy fathers, as *it is* this day.

I am convinced that God plants visions in the eyes of our heart first, before our minds because the mind is often a breeding ground for doubts and questionings. The heart is where Christ dwells and in the heart is that assurance. I had assurance of His presence of His power, of His resources and of His promise and thus, pressed into the vision for a million souls, pushing beyond any limit my young mind could conceive and saw that dreams manifest by the power of God. Thank You Jesus.

In my early years of ministry, I took nothing but the treasure He gave us the precious vision, trusting God for what I needed and trusting He would show up.

In those early days, I would seek out places where people gathered, like a magnet, the Word drew hungry, hurting people to us and Jesus healed, saved, delivered and radically transformed those that showed up, Praise God! How gratifying it has been to see God accomplish great feats amongst us. Small beginnings yes but big dreams born of the Holy Spirit into our hearts for great exploits for God. Let me encourage you do not stop dreaming and dare to dream big! God will show up, He won't disappoint! It all starts with one person being open to the possibilities God makes available. With God's hand on such endeavors, even impossible dreams are made possible and the Kingdom advances, Glory to God!

We need such vision big vision for souls. To position ourselves for it, we have to see what Jesus sees, we have to be interested in what interests Jesus and feel what Jesus feels.

The Bible says that Jesus saw the multitudes and was moved with compassion on them, scattered as they were, as sheep having no shepherd.

Matthew 9:36 But when he saw the multitudes, he was moved with compassion on them, because they fainted, and were scattered abroad, as sheep having no shepherd.

I cannot over-emphasize the importance of spending time with Jesus, in the Word, in Prayer, in Worship and surrender in the Secret Place of His presence. When our hearts are tender and receptive to the dreams of God, we open ourselves to His world of possibilities. This is where He prepares our hearts for the planting, for the fullness of the Spirit obtained in intimacy this qualifies us to receive the seed of vision. Dreams and visions are the love language of the Holy Spirit to us. Saturated in His Word and in His presence, this is where Holy Ghost fire consumed me to take the message of Christ to the ends of the earth and why I am thus compelled to reach the lost with the Gospel of Christ.

My utmost prayer is that the cross of Christ be branded upon the heart of the Body of Christ collectively and in individual hearts for lost souls.

The Lord is saying, today,
Habakkuk 1:5 Behold ye among the heathen, and regard, and wonder marvellously: for *I* will work a work in your days, *which* ye will not believe, though it be told *you.*

God's word written hundreds of years ago through the prophet Habakkuk is the Now vision for the church. The nations are calling and Revival Waves of Glory Ministries will follow the vision for an unprecedented harvest of souls for the sake of God's kingdom. As long as I breathe, I am committed to the vision of worldwide harvest, to responding to the Macedonian cry, "Come and help us." It is time to build our dreams and visions and build big in familiar and unfamiliar territory as revolutionary missionaries into His fields of divine purpose!

I want to see the release of evangelistic fervor come into the heart of God's people, to stir us to take the Gospel of Christ and mighty demonstrations of the Spirit of God into the malls, the streets into the ghetto's, the hospitals, teen hangouts, into the towns, into the cities, into the darkest continents. It is our commission and it is the ministry of Jesus. When Jesus called His twelve disciples to Him He gave them power to do the work: power over unclean spirits, to cast them out and to heal all kinds of sickness and diseases! He not only gave them power, He gave you power, He gave your children power! Consider that the power went first to the twelve. Then it saw explosive increase and leapt to 70, then to 120, then to 3,000 and then it went to as many far off as the Lord our God will call:

Acts 2:39 For the promise is unto you, and to your children, and to all that are afar off, *even* as many as the Lord our God shall call.

I can't wait until tomorrow! Why? Because I am excited about the promise of the power of

God and the Gospel, and the presence of the Holy Spirit in what He has called us to do. What more do we need to accomplish great exploits? A great exploit can be one or a million souls whatever the Lord has birthed in your heart to do. One of my missions is to especially reach women and children the masses of humanity that are being exploited. My vision is to counteract the powers of darkness, lead the exploited to Christ Jesus, free them from their captives and help elevate their physical, emotional and spiritual well-being through several outreach and mercy programs, in the Name of Jesus. As we look forward to the coming months, I will be asking God to give us clear vision for what our future will look like here at Revival Waves of Glory. For us, I sense that our first million souls will be just the beginning...a taste of a billion-soul harvest.

I am dreaming with God! Whatever His vision for us looks like, I am trusting God to lead us according to His will. I know that my heart for harvest squares with God's Word and it advances the cause of His kingdom and for sure, God always blesses dreams about soul winning! I thank God for our destiny and for yours and for the amazing plans that He desires to establish in all of our hearts in coming days. Nothing is impossible with God when we place ourselves in His hands and with harvest in full view, the greatest feats, in the name of the Lord Jesus Christ, are yet to come, in stadiums, behind the pulpit, in our own back yards, or via the world wide web. Without doubt, He will provide all that you and I need. Keep your eyes open! Both with our natural and spiritual eyes we can clearly see that indeed the fields are white unto harvest.

This is a season of amazing acceleration and we very much appreciate your prayers, support and partnership as we go out in the spirit of,

Matthew 10:7, 8 And as ye go, preach, saying, The kingdom of heaven is at hand. Heal the sick, cleanse the lepers, raise the dead, cast out devils: freely ye have received, freely give.

God Alliances

God puts people together as leaders for a purpose. We need God alliances. One of God's wonderful assurances is His promise to release a special blessing and anointing on those willing to dwell together in unity and fraternal affection.

Psalms 133:1-3 A Song of degrees of David. Behold, how good and how pleasant *it is* for brethren to dwell together in unity! *It is* like the precious ointment upon the head, that ran down upon the beard, *even* Aaron's beard: that went down to the skirts of his garments; As the dew of Hermon, *and as the dew* that descended upon the mountains of Zion: for there the LORD commanded the blessing, *even* life for evermore. Our enemy will constantly be activating false alarms to keep us in unrest.

We must keep our minds focused upon the Lord at all times. The days are difficult and trying. Much of what we have readily depended upon for day-today life will be removed. Our hope for survival in the coming seasons is a willingness to form divine alliances and friendships with others we thoroughly trust. Communication and trust will be two of the most indispensable commodities discovered in ministries and churches that flourish.

An alliance is defined as a formal agreement that establishes a relationship or partnership between other parties to achieve a particular goal. It is an association built around common interests and goals. It is primarily established to advance a certain cause or agenda. An alliance is sometimes referred to as a treaty of friendship. As 21st century Christians, we have the greatest cause of all.... to advance God's Kingdom and the revelation of Jesus Christ.

Many in the world are asking pointed questions concerning the conditions that exist in the earth. We as the church must provide the answers. It is now time for a transition to take place where we lead by example. Divine grace is being released from heaven that will allow Christians to trust one another once again. There is going to be the revelation of a high calling around which many will build their entire lives. This realization will so profoundly impact many that they will willingly lay aside personal agendas and ambitions to embrace this mandate. Great strength and advancement will be discovered by those determined to enter into such an arrangement. Divine alliances will not only produce substantial results but also a sphere of safety. The uniqueness of divine alliances allows for churches or ministries to maintain their own identity and vision while also joining in agreement with others to advance a common cause. If the Lord can find just three or four churches in a region to dwell together in harmony and support one another in friendship, then great advancement can be achieved in that territory.

The Bible also contains numerous examples of unholy alliances that were displeasing to God. These however were centered on compromise and idolatry. As always, our adversary seeks to pervert everything that is fruitful. It has been my experience that those to whom we are to be joined in covenant relationship are made evident. Marriages in ministry are very similar in this context to the marriage of man and woman. It must be a divine arrangement with those to whom we are equally yoked. Trust, communication and mutual vision are all essential ingredients that formulate a successful union. The Lord will bring into our lives those to whom we are to be joined in long-term relationship. It does not have to be something that we force into existence.

The Bible provides numerous examples of New Testament leaders who established ministry covenants. Peter and John clearly functioned as a team as discovered in Acts 9. Paul and Barnabas illustrate one of the earliest examples following the Day of Pentecost. However, one of the greatest alliances in the Bible that advanced God's because existed between David and Jonathan. Jonathan said to David, Go in safety, in as much as we have sworn to each other in the name of the Lord, saying,
1 Samuel 20:42 And Jonathan said to David, Go in peace, forasmuch as we have sworn both of us in the name of the LORD, saying, The LORD be between me and thee, and between my seed and thy seed for ever. And he arose and departed: and Jonathan went into the city.

Jonathan recognized in David the future of Israel's prosperity. There was a cause that he discovered that was worthy of sacrifice and commitment to achieve. Furthermore, the Lord imparted genuine affection in their hearts for one another. Theirs was an unbreakable bond of commitment that resulted in David's survival and Israel's welfare. The entirety of 1 Samuel 20 provides a vivid portrayal of the commitment that existed between David and Jonathan. They entered into a divine alliance that provided safety and strength. They enjoyed clear and concise communication that facilitated the plan of God and the future of Israel.

The concept of fraternal affection and brotherly love is emphasized in the ascending pyramid of graces and Godly attributes discovered in 2 Peter 1:5-8; these are essential in our quest to become one spirit with the Lord.

2 Peter 1:5-8 And beside this, giving all diligence, add to your faith virtue; and to virtue knowledge; And to knowledge temperance; and to temperance patience; and to patience godliness; And to godliness brotherly kindness; and to brotherly kindness charity.

For if these things be in you, and abound, they make *you that ye shall* neither *be* barren nor unfruitful in the knowledge of our Lord Jesus Christ.

For if these qualities are yours and are increasing, they render you neither useless nor unfruitful in the true knowledge of our Lord Jesus Christ. The Greek word for "brotherly kindness" in this passage is "Philadelphia;" It is defined as "fraternal affection; brotherly love (kindness) or love of the brethren." From a fraternal love we move forward into the "agape" of God. If it is our heart's desire to participate in the harvest of the ages and the healing of the nations, then it must be from a position of authentic compassion birthed in love. These can only be imparted to us through the Holy Spirit.

As summarized through the Apostle Paul in 1 Corinthians 13, we are to abide in faith, hope and love. We dwell in faith through the conviction and belief of man in his relationship with Heaven as well as hope, which is our confident expectation of redemption. But the greatest of these is the true affection for God and man expressed through saints; it is generated by a deposit of Heavenly virtue resident in us– LOVE.

The truth to be greatly emphasized in this generation is the transference of our lost nature for His divine nature. We have the precious and magnificent promises by which we become partakers of the divine nature and escape the corruption of this world and its lusts. By virtue of being joined with Him as His body in the mystery of incarnation, we likewise share in His heart of love and desire for the brethren as well as lost humanity.

John 17:23 I in them, and thou in me, that they may be made perfect in one; and that the world may know that thou hast sent me, and hast loved them, as thou hast loved me. We are being sent in this generation in like fashion as the Lord Himself was commissioned by His Father. We are to be carries of His heart.

I will boldly declare the current season that the body of Christ is in today. You'll be really encouraged by this as I bring forth perspective, direction and excitement concerning what God is presently doing in this hour. I will lift up God's awesome unchangeable character His ever-present help and His great faithfulness as you examine scriptures revealing how God brought His vision to birth through three great saints of old: Abraham, Zechariah and Nehemiah.

These insights are sure to both touch and torch your faith. So get ready for a change of seasons!

Changing Seasons

In every Christian's life there are seasons that change all the time. There is an awesome anointing when you know the time and season by the way of the Holy Spirit.

1 Chronicles 12:32 And of the children of Issachar, *which were men* that had understanding of the times, to know what Israel ought to do; the heads of them *were* two hundred; and all their brethren *were* at their commandment. Oh to be like the sons of Issachar, to know and understand the times and seasons and then with that wisdom, to know what to do.

For it is one thing to feel and sense the voice of God, but it's another thing to actually know what God is saying and then line up with it and do it.

Yet when we do, everything else in the natural "takes on" the word of the Lord. Think about that, because today I hear God speaking. It's time to begin decreeing the kind of season we are in. It's not a warfare season! Warfare has passed; it's a season of victories and advancement! It's a season of greater glory after one of the most difficult times of corporate and individual shaking everything that could be shaken has been shaken. Still, for some of you, maybe you're still in that battle, you're in that place. Nevertheless, I want to say that it really is springtime; it's a new day, it's a time of open heavens and it's a time of favor. In fact the hallmark of this season is "build!" Yet for many in the body of Christ lives were exactly the opposite and we were in the wilderness for a couple of years. Why? There are times when we're not ready to build. Instead we're in a time of restructuring and maintenance. It's a time of "let's hold on." That is my experience after several years of great blessing and revival.

During the past there was six weeks God said he was breaking me. He has. I was always with some money in my hands and I've had to live by faith. I had many friends and now just a couple. Different emotions surfaced. It was absolutely necessary though and He warned me: "I'm going to strip you and I'm going to break you." So you can see that it sure wasn't a season of expanding. It wasn't a season of:

"Let's bring on more staff; let's take mountains, launch projects and grow." It was a season of being in the fire. It was like fighting to stay alive. All of a sudden it was like, "Wow. I'm in a valley. It's a real dry time, a time of testing and man, I'm battling."

I know that some of you are in that same place today. Maybe it's about your health, your marriage, or your business. But whatever it is, I want to proclaim a change of the season! There's a wind of change blowing! Now you might still feel like its warfare. Nevertheless, corporately it's a time of great blessing, victory, breakthrough and advancement.

Once again I want to declare that it's a time of greater glory and the word of the Lord is Build! Build! Build! Build!

But of course there are times when you get a red light. You just don't have a release of the spirit; you don't have a commissioning. The Apostle Paul had the red light. He wanted to preach the word in Asia along with his ministry partner Silas but they were forbidden by the Holy Spirit.

Acts 6:6 Whom they set before the apostles: and when they had prayed, they laid *their* hands on them.

Sometimes you just know that you're in a holding pattern and you don't move. The light is red. So it's not always "build." Naturally there are times when the focus is on being refreshed and taking your sabbatical,

Isaiah 30:15 For thus saith the Lord GOD, the Holy One of Israel; In returning and rest shall ye be saved; in quietness and in confidence shall be your strength: and ye would not.

On the other hand there are those times when the light turns green. For Paul, after getting the red light he got the green light, the "Macedonian vision," and discerned that both he and Silas were being led by the Spirit into the district of Macedonia to minister. Yes, there are kairos times when the Spirit of God leads us into new things. I know for instance that the present time is a time to build it's a new level of building and this isn't only a word for us here at Revival Waves of Glory. There are many of you receiving the same word. Therefore, when the light is green we need to make the most of it be fruitful and multiply. In other words, take that dream God puts in our hearts and do, launch it, write it, produce it, get it out there! Because when we build according to the season and we're in tune with what God is doing and saying, the blessing is there regardless of how impossible it looks in the natural. In fact, by our determination to line up with God and by our obedience, we truly honor God. Our action is a testimony of faith and belief in the goodness of God to get the job done!

Furthermore, when the light is green, we need to ask God about the timing. For me, when I got this word to build, a sense of urgency came into my spirit to take action, no delays. That sense of urgency was not "me telling me" what to do; rather it was a quickening from the Holy Spirit and I can't help but be compelled to build quickly. Maybe in a year or two it will be a different kind of season, maybe even a season of being in a holding pattern again. Consequently I'm building NOW. It's kingdom building. We've got the green light and we're not sitting back, waiting.

My best advice is this: When you get the green light don't hold back or lose your focus. Press into the mark of your high calling with determination. Otherwise the enemy's greatest tool of distraction will throw you off course. For example, we can be so easily sidetracked by debates and disruptive behavior (and more), instead of being focused on God's highway of holiness and purpose.

John 9:4 I must work the works of him that sent me, while it is day: the night cometh, when no man can work. Make a decree regardless of what's going on in your circumstances. Claim: THIS IS A TIME OF OPEN HEAVENS, GREATER GLORY, ADVANCE AND MULTIPLY AND IT'S A TIME FOR BUILDING. BUILDING AND MOVING FORWARD CHANGE Right now I'm focused on building infrastructure and getting as big and as massive as we can. That's where my heart is. I'm expanding in my Spirit, dreaming.

I call it "visionating." Visionating is a gift; it's an impartation from God. You see, God wants us to be fruitful and He wants us to be successful. He wants us to be the head and He wants twelve baskets leftover.

John 6:11-13 And Jesus took the loaves; and when he had given thanks, he distributed to the disciples, and the disciples to them that were set down; and likewise of the fishes as much as they would. When they were filled, he said unto his disciples, Gather up the fragments that remain, that nothing be lost. Therefore they gathered *them* together, and filled twelve baskets with the fragments of the five barley loaves, which remained over and above unto them that had eaten. He's a God of overflow, abundance and blessing; and so we need to be that way in our visionating and in our dreams. Anything is possible with God. Could it be that some of you need to ask God to deal with a mindset that limits Him? If that's you, let this prophetic word through the prophet Isaiah challenge you.

Isaiah 54:2, 3 Enlarge the place of thy tent, and let them stretch forth the curtains of thine habitations: spare not, lengthen thy cords, and strengthen thy stakes; For thou shalt break forth on the right hand and on the left; and thy seed shall inherit the Gentiles, and make the desolate cities to be inhabited.

The fact is, building and moving forward = change. Nothing stays the same. Are you ready in your own life for nothing to be the same as it was? Taking a step of faith based on what God has put in our hearts is truly great, yet we also need to remember to be practical. Yes, visionating brings vision. But in practical terms, structure and resources are necessary to build that vision. As a matter of fact, many of you are wondering just how to get started. Or you are already in the process but you're asking how to move to the next level. Often we just don't understand how to begin or how to advance to the next stage. We're going to study our road map: the Bible.

Together as we look at how God cast His vision and then helped different saints of old like Abraham, Zachariah and Nehemiah fulfill it, I know many of you will be as encouraged and pumped up as I am about what He is doing in this hour. And He wants to work through us! Wow!

Luke 1:45 And blessed *is* she that believed: for there shall be a performance of those things which were told her from the Lord.

Yeah! It's a change of season alright! Hallelujah! God is casting vision and you're in for big blessings. Believe it.... "Because when we build according to the season and we're in tune with what God is doing and saying, the blessings are there regardless of how impossible it looks in the natural. In fact, by our determination to line up with God and by our obedience, we truly honor God. Our action is a testimony of faith and belief in the goodness of God to get the job done!"

I know that God has spoken too many of you about your life, your call, your destiny, your purpose and your ministry, yet your dreams and visions are unfulfilled. Often the truth of the matter simply comes down to actually taking the first step. So let's dig into the Bible and discover some pertinent keys that will help you get started in fulfilling God's vision and equally, how to take step two so that you can move on to the next level. Yes, it's time to get uncomfortable and charter those unknown waters! You might not know exactly where you're going, but head out with God anyway. You are going to get there:
Hebrews 11:8 By faith Abraham, when he was called to go out into a place which he should after receive for an inheritance, obeyed; and he went out, not knowing whither he went. So let's check out Abraham's faith adventure.

First let me remind you that Abraham's former name was Abram. God changed it to Abraham after this story,

Genesis 17:5 Neither shall thy name any more be called Abram, but thy name shall be Abraham; for a father of many nations have I made thee.

Now, beginning in Genesis 15:1 I want you to understand the context

Genesis 15:1 After these things the word of the LORD came unto Abram in a vision, saying, Fear not, Abram: I *am* thy shield, *and* thy exceeding great reward.

Here we see that God had already spoken to Abram, but now He wants to establish, build up and strengthen His prophetic word. God accomplished this by speaking to Abram again, but differently, this time in a vision.

Why a vision? It's because God does something in a person's heart by visions. God wants to establish vision. Yet some of you have shut down that dreaming, vision place with God. You're worried that it's just your own thoughts, your own hopes or dreams. It's supposed to be your thoughts, your hopes and your dreams. God wants to be with you in the midst of your thoughts, hopes and dreams; it's a process. We need to begin to

dream. In part one I shared about "visionating," that it's a gift from God; an impartation. I visionate and I dream about souls. I dream about ministry. I dream about buildings, finances and resources, structure. So in Abram's vision God immediately dealt with his heart: "Do not be afraid, Abram. I am your shield, your exceedingly great reward."
It is then that Abram freely complains (paraphrase):
Genesis 15:2 And Abram said, Lord GOD, what wilt thou give me, seeing I go childless, and the steward of my house *is* this Eliezer of Damascus?

And people will say to me, "Bill, all this vision is great, but how does it work practically?" Hold that question. (Back to Abram.) God hears his plea and says:
Genesis 15:4 And, behold, the word of the LORD *came* unto him, saying, This shall not be thine heir; but he that shall come forth out of thine own bowels shall be thine heir.

Next, immediately God makes his prophet word real by taking Abram outside and showing him something:
Genesis 15:5 And he brought him forth abroad, and said, Look now toward heaven,

and tell the stars, if thou be able to number them: and he said unto him, So shall thy seed be.

In other words God is saying: "Abram! Look, behold, see, dream, look towards heaven, count the stars if you are able to number them. So shall your descendants be. Get it in your spirit. I want you to think about what I am about to do. Think about the descendants that are going to be yours. Meditate on the promise. Let me give you a key to receiving the heir. God said come on out here and dream. Before there was an "expected outcome" God said: "Now look." And Abram looks up into the heavens and begins to count the stars... maybe he gets to a million stars and then he realizes, so shall my descendants be. He grasps that he can't count that high; it's so exceedingly, abundantly above what he could even think, ask or imagine. Now don't miss this. A holy moment: It's here that Abram believed God. Step one, accomplished. He believed the vision. Let's bring this closer to home. God wants to take you outside and say, "Look see, dream." Yet so often we get so focused on what we don't have.

My advice is: Don't be afraid to dream; be a dreamer; begin to meditate, begin to imagine; begin to have Holy Ghost, sanctified fantasies about what God is speaking to you. Take step one and believe God. Believe the vision that God is downloading into your heart. Now let's take a look at how God moved Zerubbabel and his people from step one to step two.

Outlined in the Book of Zechariah Chapters 1-3, we see that the prophet Zechariah receives prophetic words (from the angel of the Lord) of encouragement, direction and confirmation concerning Jerusalem and rebuilding the Second Temple. In particular, Chapter 4 includes prophetic words for Zerubbabel, the grandson of Jehoiachin who was granted permission from Cyrus, the king of Persia, to return to Israel. He went in the first wave along with other exiled Jews after 70 years of Babylonian captivity to rebuild the Temple.

However, the construction work for the Second Temple came to a standstill. (Ezra Chapter Four.) Zerubbabel was greatly discouraged by this and therefore Zechariah's message was vital.

Zechariah 1:6-9 But my words and my statutes, which I commanded my servants the prophets, did they not take hold of your fathers? and they returned and said, Like as the LORD of hosts thought to do unto us, according to our ways, and according to our doings, so hath he dealt with us. Upon the four and twentieth day of the eleventh month, which *is* the month Sebat, in the second year of Darius, came the word of the LORD unto Zechariah, the son of Berechiah, the son of Iddo the prophet, saying, I saw by night, and behold a man riding upon a red horse, and he stood among the myrtle trees that *were* in the bottom; and behind him *were there* red horses, speckled, and white. Then said I, O my lord, what *are* these? And the angel that talked with me said unto me, I will shew thee what these *be*.

Also for double confirmation, we see that the prophet Haggai received (from God) an exhortation for Zerubbabel and the remnant living in Jerusalem: They must stop thinking only about themselves and begin building the Temple, said the Lord. Consequently a Godly fear came upon everyone to obey God and their spirits were stirred to get to work on the house of the Lord.

Haggai 1:13, 14 Then spake Haggai the LORD'S messenger in the LORD'S message unto the people, saying, I *am* with you, saith the LORD. And the LORD stirred up the spirit of Zerubbabel the son of Shealtiel, governor of Judah, and the spirit of Joshua the son of Josedech, the high priest, and the spirit of all the remnant of the people; and they came and did work in the house of the LORD of hosts, their God, Notice the beautiful words of Ezra,

Ezra 7:11 Now this *is* the copy of the letter that the king Artaxerxes gave unto Ezra the priest, the scribe, *even* a scribe of the words of the commandments of the LORD, and of his statutes to Israel.

The prophets clearly encouraged Zerubbabel to see the building project through to the end.

Ezra 5:2 Then rose up Zerubbabel the son of Shealtiel, and Jeshua the son of Jozadak, and began to build the house of God which *is* at Jerusalem: and with them *were* the prophets of God helping them.

Ezra 6:14 And the elders of the Jews builded, and they prospered through the prophesying of Haggai the prophet and Zechariah the son of Iddo. And they builded, and finished *it,* according to the commandment of the God of Israel, and according to the commandment of Cyrus, and Darius, and Artaxerxes king of Persia.

There would have been no re-building of the Temple without the prophets helping and supporting them without them prophesying! There are too many ministries, churches and people trying to build without the true prophets helping them!

We can never really build and get where God wants us to go without supernatural encounters, dreams, visions, open heavens and prophecies, given by visionaries and seer-prophets. We need those in the midst of the building. If you want to be successful in ministry you need to have the constant prophetic anointing available to influence your life. In fact, we've got to have a "prophetic culture." Prophetic teams, teams of the supernatural, seers and visionaries. I want to surround myself here at Revival Waves of Glory, for example, prophetic people who will speak what God is saying. Zerubbabel and the people prospered according to the prophesying. They believed the true prophetic voices that God spoke through. That's step two! That's one main key to help you move on to the next level. When your life, ministry, church and family do not have the prophesying, the prospering stops. That is why ministries get old and stale.

They are heavy on the pastoral and teaching but they don't have enough of the prophesying. We need to have that anointing influencing our lives; those Christians who can move prophetically and speak into our lives accordingly. We need to be exposed to this realm, and as I mentioned before, we need to have that culture. Actually the culture is apostolic because everything that God does is built on the foundation of the apostles and prophets.

Ephesians 2:20 And are built upon the foundation of the apostles and prophets, Jesus Christ himself being the chief corner *stone;*

Apostles (builders) and prophets (seers), by God's design, naturally partner and work together. If we don't have the prophetic men and women teamed with apostolic men and women then we won't have real success or prosperity when it comes to seeing the vision truly fulfilled.

We're going to discover several keys about what it takes to be an apostle and the important role of apostles in God's building plan by examining a portion of Nehemiah's life. In fact, I am feeding on the Books of Nehemiah, Zechariah, Ezra and Haggai!

Nehemiah actually pictures what a true, trustworthy apostle should look like. If the apostles that God is raising up today would press in for the same king of integrity and devotion that Nehemiah had, then the body of Christ could relax more and begin to trust the modern-day apostles more. We see that Nehemiah was still in captivity, living in Susa, when he received the bad news that Jerusalem's walls were burned with fire, the gates were broken down and the people there were in great reproach.

Nehemiah 1:1-4 The words of Nehemiah the son of Hachaliah. And it came to pass in the month Chisleu, in the twentieth year, as I was in Shushan the palace, That Hanani, one of my brethren, came, he and *certain* men of Judah; and I asked them concerning the Jews

that had escaped, which were left of the captivity, and concerning Jerusalem. And they said unto me, the remnants that are left of the captivity there in the province *are* in great affliction and reproach: the wall of Jerusalem also *is* broken down, and the gates thereof are burned with fire. And it came to pass, when I heard these words, that I sat down and wept, and mourned *certain* days, and fasted, and prayed before the God of heaven,
His grief was great and in that state he postured himself before God after a time of fasting and prayer, confessing the sins of his people and asking God for favor with the king.

Nehemiah 1:5-11 And said, I beseech thee, O LORD God of heaven, the great and terrible God, that keepeth covenant and mercy for them that love him and observe his commandments: Let thine ear now be attentive, and thine eyes open, that thou mayest hear the prayer of thy servant, which I pray before thee now, day and night, for the children of Israel thy servants, and confess the sins of the children of Israel, which we have sinned against thee: both I and my father's house have sinned. We have dealt very corruptly against thee, and have not kept the commandments, nor the statutes, nor the judgments, which thou commandedst thy servant Moses. Remember, I beseech thee, the word that thou commandedst thy servant Moses, saying, *If* ye transgress, I will scatter you abroad among the nations: But *if* ye turn unto me, and keep my commandments, and do them; though there were of you cast out unto the uttermost part of the heaven, *yet* will I gather them from thence, and will bring them unto the place that I have chosen to set my name there. Now these *are* thy servants and thy people, whom thou hast redeemed by thy great power, and by thy strong hand. O Lord, I beseech thee, let now thine ear be attentive to the prayer of thy servant, and to the prayer of thy servants, who desire to fear thy name: and prosper, I pray thee, thy servant this day, and grant him mercy in the sight of this man. For I was the king's cupbearer.

How important is fasting and praying? There is nothing done without prayer. It is absolutely crucial to gaining the victory in spiritual warfare so that you can receive God's heart and keep moving forward no matter how difficult it is. Why did Nehemiah need the king's favor? Because he wanted to do more than just weep. God is looking for believers today who will do more than weep, who will do more than complain. He is looking for people who will seek His favor, the favor of the King of Kings and the Lord of Lords! People, who will fast, pray and press in with all their might. Naturally when Nehemiah came before the king, his sad face caused the king to enquire about his sorrow. Immediately the opportunity to speak his heart arose as the king asked him:

Nehemiah 2:4, 5 Then the king said unto me, For what dost thou make request? So I prayed to the God of heaven. It was at that moment Nehemiah prayed and then with a ready answer he asked: And I said unto the king, If it please the king, and if thy servant have found favour in thy sight, that thou wouldest send me unto Judah, unto the city of my fathers' sepulchres, that I may build it.

Nehemiah, the cupbearer, wanted to be sent out to rebuild. He was just a cupbearer, right? He wasn't one of the King's advisors, a great politician or anyone who looked important. Yet he knew his authority and he assessed the situation in Jerusalem. Not thrown off by the terrible news, his apostolic mindset took over and he said to himself: I'm up to the challenge. He wasn't overwhelmed by how impossible the situation was; instead he said to himself: I'm going to do something about this. Commissioned by God and not self-appointed, he wanted the full backing and written endorsement of the king in a letter.

Nehemiah 2:7 Moreover I said unto the king, If it please the king, let letters be given me to the governors beyond the river, that they may convey me over till I come into Judah;

Anyone who would dispute with him would have to answer to the king! In fact, when he was ready to leave for Jerusalem he had the king's letter, officers of the army and horsemen.

Nehemiah 2:9 Then I came to the governors beyond the river, and gave them the king's letters. Now the king had sent captains of the army and horsemen with me.

If you're a true apostolic man or woman, you understand that you're not apostolic unless you are sent (by a governing body like a church) and commissioned by a word from heaven. It means you're a dreamer, a visionary and a builder. Furthermore, it doesn't matter if you are a business person, a housewife, a dishwasher, a construction worker, a school teacher, or a cupbearer, if it's God's plan, you are as eligible as anyone to receive an apostolic call.

An apostolic man or woman is up to the challenge to rebuild, repair and raise up what's broken down. There might only be twenty people left in a church and it's in debt, every other pastor has given up, but you're up to the challenge. You want to be there. The darker the better, the harder it is, the more you like the challenge, because you have a vision! You see beyond the circumstances. You see tomorrow and what God has promised. Back to Nehemiah, when he arrived in Jerusalem, taking what God put in his heart and a few trusted men he stealthily inspected the walls.

Nehemiah 2:12 And I arose in the night, I and some few men with me; neither told I *any* man what my God had put in my heart to do at Jerusalem: neither *was there any* beast with me, save the beast that I rode upon. Then he reported his findings to the people along with the testimony about how the hand of God had been favorable toward him.

Equally, after repeating the king's words to all the people, they all said,
Nehemiah 2:18 Then I told them of the hand of my God which was good upon me; as also the king's words that he had spoken unto me. And they said, Let us rise up and build. So they strengthened their hands for *this* good *work*. That is all it takes to get started. A few people and what God has placed in your heart. Now the enemy was shocked when they heard about Israel's plans and they began an unrelenting campaign of attack by mocking them; intimidate and strike fear into their hearts.

Nehemiah 4:1 But it came to pass, that when Sanballat heard that we builded the wall, he was wroth, and took great indignation, and mocked the Jews.

Nehemiah 4:8-12 And conspired all of them together to come *and* to fight against Jerusalem, and to hinder it. Nevertheless we made our prayer unto our God, and set a watch against them day and night, because of them. And Judah said, The strength of the bearers of burdens is decayed, and *there is* much rubbish; so that we are not able to build the wall. And our adversaries said, They shall not know, neither see, till we come in the midst among them, and slay them, and cause the work to cease. And it came to pass, that when the Jews which dwelt by them came, they said unto us ten times, From all places whence ye shall return unto us *they will be upon you.* Yet all their schemes were no match for Nehemiah's divine strategy. He set armed workers with guards to protect them; he placed trumpeters to sound the alarm when necessary. As the people continued to build, his battle plan stood in place. But the enemy was not going to give up. Four letters were sent to Nehemiah trying to arrange a meeting.

Nehemiah 6:2-4 That Sanballat and Geshem sent unto me, saying, Come, let us meet together in *some one of* the villages in the plain of Ono. But they thought to do me mischief. And I sent messengers unto them, saying, I *am* doing a great work, so that I cannot come down: why should the work cease, whilst I leave it, and come down to you? Yet they sent unto me four times after this sort; and I answered them after the same manner. Wisely Nehemiah was not drawn away from the final phase of rebuilding the walls. After the first letter, point blank he fired back: "I am doing a great work, so that I cannot come down. Why should the work cease while I leave it and go down to you?" People, we can't be distracted. Don't let the schemes of the enemy, be it false accusations, rumors, gossip, or even flattery get you off course. Today we don't have time to "come down off the wall" because it's a change of seasons and it's time to build. I'm focused. There's no way anyone can distract Bill Vincent now. I'm building and I'm full steam ahead. I don't have time for yesterdays. Don't let yesterday's hurts, old baggage, insecurities, or fear, stop you. Have a mind to work. Be focused on the vision God has given you. Whatever you put your hand to, don't take it off; don't stop until the work is finished. Push it all the way through.

Take a step, move, advance, run, no looking back. Let God touch and torch your faith to believe that He is with you every step of the way just like He was with Abraham, Zechariah, Haggai, Ezra and Nehemiah. He is cheering you on, always all the time, never stopping. God is for you, so nothing can prevail against you!

Breakthrough Revival

Revival has been diminished to a word not what it is meant to be. God is releasing a breakthrough revival. There have been prophetic people who have seen an angel that stated his name is "Breakthrough" and he has been assigned to the United States. The Revelatory realm is opening. I had an angel appear to me in the Litchfield Revival and He said, "My name is Breakthrough and I have now been assigned to the United States." This angel revealed historical accounts of past revivals that transpired to God's glory that he was involved in. His job is to release breakthrough and awakening to initiate a wave of harvest by extracting all obstacles to God's plans while the other angels gather the harvest. God reminded me of this and began to speak to me.

God said that for two years He has been laying the groundwork for the next revival. A revival, He said, that present stadiums are not adequate to hold once it is fully manifested.

Very often we have a mistaken notion that we must spend extended periods of time in prayer and fasting for the Lord to speak to us in clear and concise ways. Naturally, that is a good way to position ourselves before God's Throne to hear from Him. Nevertheless, the Lord also chooses to speak in ways that sometimes surprises us. The Lord will often speak to us in the midst of a storm, while in a great trial or even after a long day.

Some from heaven's host are fierce and overwhelming in appearance, but these seemed tender and loving. End-Time provision angels gather where God is!

Matthew 13:37-43 He answered and said unto them, He that soweth the good seed is the Son of man; The field is the world; the good seed are the children of the kingdom; but the tares are the children of the wicked *one;* The enemy that sowed them is the devil; the harvest is the end of the world; and the reapers are the angels. As therefore the tares are gathered and burned in the fire; so shall it be in the end of this world. The Son of man shall send forth his angels, and they shall gather out of his kingdom all things that offend, and them which do iniquity; And shall cast them into a furnace of fire: there shall be wailing and gnashing of teeth. Then shall the righteous shine forth as the sun in the kingdom of their Father. Who hath ears to hear, let him hear.

Jesus said so in this passage. It is a clear outline of the spiritual conflict that will exist in the days immediately preceding His return.

In Matthew 13 the Lord gives the following interpretation involving the latter-day generation saying, He said, "The one who sows the good seed is the Son of Man and the field is the world; and as for the good seed, these are the sons of the kingdom; and the tares are the sons of the evil one; and the enemy who sowed them is the devil, and the harvest is the end of the age; and the reapers are angels. So just as the tares are gathered up and burned with fire, so shall it be at the end of the age. The Bible plainly articulates that the field in which the Lord has sown good seed is the world. The one who sows the good seed is the Son of Man. The seed that He imparts are the children of the Kingdom. The Lord Jesus Himself clearly states that there are a host of angels designated for the end-time generation who will work collectively with

God's people in the labor of the last-day harvest. "Angels that gather" will not only collect the wheat into the barn but also extract stumbling blocks that interfere with the flourishing of God's Kingdom.

Those used most prominently in this installment of God's plan will not boast in their wisdom or might, but in knowing the Lord intimately.

Jeremiah 9:23, 24 Thus saith the LORD, Let not the wise *man* glory in his wisdom, neither let the mighty *man* glory in his might, let not the rich *man* glory in his riches: But let him that glorieth glory in this, that he understandeth and knoweth me, that I *am* the LORD which exercise lovingkindness, judgment, and righteousness, in the earth: for in these *things* I delight, saith the LORD.

It is the Lord's intent during this season to fully mobilize the Body of Christ into its function as God's intermediary on the Earth. The foremost responsibility of the five-fold ministry is to equip God's people to do the work of the ministry. Even the feeblest among us should be as noble and victorious as the great worshiping-warrior, King David.

Zechariah 12:8 In that day shall the LORD defend the inhabitants of Jerusalem; and he that is feeble among them at that day shall be as David; and the house of David *shall be* as God, as the angel of the LORD before them. It also articulated our directive to move in faith on the earth in order to cooperate in the Spirit with this Heavenly host.

This is an end-time strategy that is to be employed now. The Predominant Scripture to be utilized in this commissioning is Matthew 10:7-8 declaring,
Matthew 10:7, 8 And as ye go, preach, saying, The kingdom of heaven is at hand. Heal the sick, cleanse the lepers, raise the dead, cast out devils: freely ye have received, freely give. This will be a season of harvest; a harvest of souls and a harvest of promises. Even so, it will come not by the mere articulation of words but also with power.

In Exodus 23 God promised to send an Angel before Israel to overcome every enemy and establish them in the land of promise.

Their obedience to the Word assured their victory and released the Lord to remove sickness from their midst. In like fashion, a wave of healing will accompany this season of grace we are now entering.

The presence of these angels will be very similar to the spiritual sign given to King David in his battle with the Philistines in Second Samuel 5. When David inquired of the Lord for divine strategy and precise timing, the Lord released "breakthrough" to route all opposition to grant a complete victory! The scripture emphasizes that, David came to Baal-perazim and defeated them there; and he said, "The LORD has broken through my enemies before me like the breakthrough of waters." Therefore he named that place Baalperazim. (The master of breakthrough.) Victory is achieved in the spirit realm first and then manifested in the natural realm.

In the continuation of this prophetic scenario, the Bible tells us David knew to move against his enemies when he discerned wind blowing among the balsam trees. Following that example, we will learn in this day to co-operate with the Lord's timing when we discern God's winds, His angels, moving on our behalf. There will be cooperation between heaven and earth in this powerful dynamic.

Hebrews 1:7 And of the angels he saith, Who maketh his angels spirits, and his ministers a flame of fire. The end-time church will learn to cooperate fully with the spiritual host assigned to us as friends learn to cohesively work in unison with their closest friends. It is our responsibility to meticulously follow the Holy Spirit's leadership to fully activate every spiritual dynamic and resource allotted to us. We release on the earth what we discern in the Spirit.

Genesis 38:27-30 And it came to pass in the time of her travail, that, behold, twins *were* in her womb. And it came to pass, when she travailed, that *the one* put out *his* hand: and the midwife took and bound upon his hand a scarlet thread, saying, This came out first. And it came to pass, as he drew back his hand, that, behold, his brother came out: and she said, How hast thou broken forth? *this* breach *be* upon thee: therefore his name was called Pharez. And afterward came out his brother, that had the scarlet thread upon his hand: and his name was called Zarah.

In this passage we discover the birthing of Judah's twins. If we are to qualify to be utilized in this spiritual move we must possess

boldness and determination. It would be a breach for us to put our hand to this task and then draw it back. According to,
Hebrews 10:37-39 For yet a little while, and he that shall come will come, and will not tarry. Now the just shall live by faith: but if *any man* draw back, my soul shall have no pleasure in him. But we are not of them who draw back unto perdition; but of them that believe to the saving of the soul.

We cannot be among those who drawback because of opposition or fear, but rather among those who press forward to see breakthrough achieved.

Embracing our opportunity we have arrived at a "fullness of time" juncture of church history. God's end-time plan is being set in motion. Naturally, this is not the only thing that He is doing but it is certainly a vital part. Our role is to continue to pursue the simplicity and purity of devotion to Christ Jesus and become men and women of prayer. This empowers the spiritual host to battle on our behalf in the spiritual realm to achieve notable victories to the Lord's glory. There is a spiritual principle that states where evil abounds, grace does much more abound. Clearly our nation is in trouble.

Nevertheless, the Lord is extending an incredible opportunity for His greatgrace. We must embrace every divine opportunity and employ these incredible gifts being delegated to us at this crucial moment.

Birthing God's Champions

There is a new breed of saints rising up in this hour. Are you ready to be a champion for God right now! Hang on for what is coming. Micah 4:9, 10 Now why dost thou cry out aloud? *is there* no king in thee? Is thy counsellor perished? for pangs have taken thee as a woman in travail. Be in pain, and labour to bring forth, O daughter of Zion, like a woman in travail: for now shalt thou go forth out of the city, and thou shalt dwell in the field, and thou shalt go *even* to Babylon; there shalt thou be delivered; there the LORD shall redeem thee from the hand of thine enemies.

Becoming a spiritual champion simply means yielding ourselves so that the Great Champion of Heaven can express Himself through us.

Moses gave up the luxury and extravagant lifestyle of Egypt in order to bear the reproach and identity of God's people. In so doing he initiated a spiritual principle. The more fully one yields in sacrificially giving themselves to the identity of Jesus, the greater the spiritual opportunity. Our call is to be the representation of Heaven on earth. From among the nations of the earth God chose Israel...from among the Israelites God identified the tribe of Levi. Furthermore, from the tribe of Levi the Lord awarded the descendants of Zadok a special place at His table because of their loyalty and faithfulness during times of apostasy and infidelity. This reality points to the remnant of a remnant of a remnant. Those who remain constant and dedicated to the anointing of God receive a specific blessing of grace and favor. Endowments of His Spirit will be imparted to empower us to overcome the oppressions of this world and become the representation of Heaven on earth.

In the midst of a society characterized by Babylonian confusion, a body of believers will emerge having become victorious who embody the virtues of the "overcomers." The Bible declares that the Lord jealously desires the anointing He has placed within us.

James 4:5 Do ye think that the scripture saith in vain, The spirit that dwelleth in us lusteth to envy? Resident within the heart of the Father is His thoughts for this generation. The Spirit searches the depths of God's heart to reveal the hidden secrets of His plans and purposes.

God said "time for time is measured." In the same fashion that we measure the height and width of something with a measuring rod so also has the Father measured an allotment of time in order to accomplish His plan of redemption. While He views the beginning of the measuring rod He could also see the end.

At the same moment that he examined the creation and life of Adam He also viewed the latter days and the generation ordained to live in the end time. While He was viewing the life of the Patriarchs he was also examining the latter day leaders who would carry His anointing for His grand finale. He knew the end from the beginning and specifically imparted a seed of destiny into the hearts of a generation to emerge at the end of time to become the champions of Heaven. Before He ever fashioned the earth He foresaw an "overcoming" generation who would embody His nature and power. From this posture of sovereignty, the Lord ordained a plan of victory that we are now beginning to experience. That is His plan of destiny. God says that the grand finale is about to begin.

Inhabitant in one of the most often quoted stories in the Bible it's a profound spiritual reality with direct application for today.

In John 4 the Bible records one of the most phenomenal encounters with the Lord Jesus and a woman to whom the Scriptures do not give a name we only know her as the woman at the well. What an incredible privilege that was given to this precious woman to have a face-to-face encounter with the King of Glory. On this fateful day the Lord sent his disciples away and waited at a well for this little lady to make her routine visit to draw water. One can only speculate if this precious woman knew if something uniquely qualified this day as one of the most phenomenal in her life. We can only wonder if that morning seemed odd or unique when she was awakened to the eastern sun. Without question, that day marked appoint of demarcation in her life and transformed not only her. But an entire city. All the days the Lord walked the earth were ordained and specifically orchestrated by the Holy Spirit. Therefore we confidently recognize the strategy of Heaven in the awakening of the remarkable destiny inhabitant in this precious woman on this fateful day.

Before the foundation of the world, a seed of destiny was imparted into this woman that was to be awakened in a unique fashion

Ephesians 1:4 According as he hath chosen us in him before the foundation of the world, that we should be holy and without blame before him in love:

The Lord has made it profoundly clear to us that this encounter is a prophetic model for the awakening of the Western Church in this generation. In many ways, the Western Church can be characterized with the life of this woman. It seems we have been married to many things except the very purpose for which we were created. We have married denominations, movements and different expressions of revival and failed to join ourselves to the One who sent these awakenings to us. The day has now arrived; however, those seeds of destiny are to be inflamed through the model demonstrated in John Chapter 4.

The Lord could have chosen any of His power to capture the attention of this woman. However, he simply articulated the secrets of her heart and accomplished the will of the

Father. The meeting at the well was not a random encounter. It was divinely orchestrated in order to awaken within this woman a see of destiny imparted to her before the foundation of the world. The Lord had an appointment with this woman to bring her to the awareness of her destiny. To her was given one of the greatest privileges ever bestowed upon an individual face-to-face conversation with the King of Glory. What an awesome privilege! It is significant that the Lord utilized His revelatory knowledge to awaken this woman to the purpose of Heaven.

This prophetic model will also awaken the Western Church to her destiny! The Lord Jesus engaged the revelatory realm of Heaven to access the seed of destiny resident in this woman although covered with failure, disillusionment and shame.

It is impossible for us to become spiritual champions relying upon our own strength and virtue. Spiritual victory is the result of an impartation from heaven allowing the Lord to express His virtue and characteristics through an overcoming body of believers.

Her exclamation that she knew a Messiah would someday come to reveal the secrets of the heart and do supernatural things expressed the foreknown seed of destiny. Like the woman at the well, when the Western Church experiences the revelatory realm of heaven that displays the secrets of the heart according to Hebrews 4:12, it will likewise awaken her to supernatural faith that will win our nation. For the word of God is living and active and sharper than any two edged sword piercing as far as the division of soul and spirit, of both joints and marrow and able to judge the thoughts and intentions of the heart.

And there is no creature hidden from His sight, but all things are open and lay bare to the eyes of Him with whom we have to do.

Hebrews 4:12, 13 For the word of God *is* quick, and powerful, and sharper than any twoedged sword, piercing even to the dividing asunder of soul and spirit, and of the joints and marrow, and *is* a discerner of the thoughts and intents of the heart. Neither is there any creature that is not manifest in his sight: but all things *are* naked and opened unto the eyes of him with whom we have to do. This woman became an awesome evangelist because of the supernatural faith imparted to her by her encounter at the well. Clearly she had previously known the sorrow of shame and failure yet the Lord recognized a great destiny that could only have been supernaturally discerned. This woman was the Lord's choice to awaken the area of Samaria to a day of visitation. The Bible tells us that the entire city came out to hear the testimony of Christ because of the word of this woman.

Our primary purpose is to identify the hidden seed of destiny inherent the champions of this generation. They presently do not have the appearance or restart of a champion but like this little woman, they carry a seed of purpose and destiny that will be awakened to spiritual greatness. It is the Living Word being manifested who reveals and discerns the thoughts and intents of the heart distinguishing spirit and soul. That is the revelatory realm of Heaven! All things are open and lay bare before the One to Whom we have to do; there is nothing hidden from His sight. However, when manifested, it will reap the same benefits as it did with the Samaritan village. This woman became a champion of Heaven because of her encounter with the Lord at the well. The Lord

Jesus is the Light of the World. When His light strikes the seeds of destiny inherent in a generation it will awaken them to a life of victory and an army of champions will emerge. His revelatory light of His end-time plan is being revealed and igniting the souls of people to become the champions they have been ordained to be.

Apostolic Revolution

God has been looking at the Body of Christ, to see if there will be a rise of new Church Government. There is a coming revolution like the Church has never seen. God is raising up training centers all over America. Revival Waves of Glory is starting one of these centers at a small scale. We are just doing what God is speaking. I believe it will be the first of at least 100 centers in the coming years.

God is not just planting churches, He is planting Apostolic Centers! During the last few years of ministry I've been in numerous places where the Holy Spirit said, "I want you to prophesy about the emerging apostolic centers and what they look like."

In this strategic hour, a call is going out to many believers to take their place in this sphere. You, yes, you, may be led by the Holy Spirit to join with others. Corporately, to focus on facilitating this whole new thing that the Holy Spirit is wanting to do in the Body of

Christ today. A center may well be located in your city or region, or in your nation. I'll speak briefly, once again, about apostolic centers under new Government, New Structure towards the end of this chapter.

I must ask this burning question, "Are you aware that we are in a move of God?" I think it's surprising, the number of believers today, who are still waiting for this move to begin. I am making an announcement: "We are in one. It's still coming, but we are in it." The moment we begin to accept this, even before we can really give "language" to what it all means, is the moment we are in a better position to take more responsibility for it.

Therefore, what I am attempting here today is to begin laying a prophetic grid of framework, to describe this move, so that we can take more responsibility for it. I'm seeing it like the crest of this next wave tsunami wave. The healing and the prayer movements are in this wave, but it's bigger than this. What's happening today in evangelism and the great harvest doesn't complete the picture either! I believe these three major moves of God (healing, prayer movement, and evangelism harvest) will come together and constitute one, global move. This fusion gives life and substance to the tsunami wave or move of God, but we must not box God in; we have to give Him freedom to speak/release more into this wave. I will speak about the slightly different perspective on this global move later under The Tabernacle of David. I want to also add that this move of God probably comes under the umbrella of the apostolic. But what does that mean? There are so many variables that take place within this context.

Also, we hear so much "buzz" about apostolic churches, apostolic networks and the apostles; we have so many buzz words in the church today. However, a strong sense of anticipation is stirring within us about this whole new model/face that is coming to the church. But, we need a true understanding of what this is going to look like because it's going to influence and change how we will do church. Plus, when the anointing comes to activate this new thing and it's not even here in maturity right now there are going to be some specific anointings released with it. At this point, I would now like to continue with an overview of several characteristics of the apostle and highlight nine true signs of what qualified genuine apostolic anointing and authority looks like.

An apostle is the missionary who first plants the Christian faith in any part of the world and one who initiates any great moral reform, or who advocates any important belief.

An apostle must be chosen and appointed by God. There are God-made apostles, but unfortunately, there are man-made apostles, too. We need God-made apostles who are prepared, anointed, authorized and sent by Him. Therefore, an apostle must never be appointed by any man or college, institution or church that might want to do so based solely on their own initiative, separate from the direction of the Holy Spirit; an apostle must not be self-appointed. God is restoring apostles in the church today, but I would like to pause and bring a word of caution. Those who say "I am an apostle" are the ones that we need to be careful of. Usually the ones that really are apostles don't say anything about who they are. The anointing speaks for itself. And when the anointing is there that's it! Also, there are those who may have the anointing on their life for the apostolic, but it may only be for a group of ten in their apostolic sphere.

Therefore, they wouldn't carry themselves as an apostle into the world at that level.

In addition, there is another principle I will attempt to explain when a prophet is not received (as a prophet).

Matthew 10:41 He that receiveth a prophet in the name of a prophet shall receive a prophet's reward; and he that receiveth a righteous man in the name of a righteous man shall receive a righteous man's reward.

Whoever does not receive the true prophet will forfeit the reward that comes with the gift the prophet bears, but having said that, everyone is not going to receive the prophet in that office because the prophet is not meant to be everyone's prophet, (just as the apostle is neither everyone's apostle, nor the evangelist everyone's evangelist). In addition, it is my belief that to even qualify to use the name "apostle," every person who has an apostolic network should be moving in some kind of miracles, signs and wonders and mighty deeds.

I want to share with you, true signs of what qualified genuine apostolic anointing and authority looks like:

Separation
Believers are instructed by God to abandon themselves to a lifestyle of consecration; those who will be totally separated to His purpose and call. Consecration demands a high commitment to holiness and true apostles will reflect his way of life.

Romans 1:1 Paul, a servant of Jesus Christ, called *to be* an apostle, separated unto the gospel of God,

Fathering

True apostolic anointing is like being a loving father and is reproductive, producing mature sons and daughters.

1 Corinthians 4:15 For though ye have ten thousand instructors in Christ, yet *have ye* not many fathers: for in Christ Jesus I have begotten you through the gospel.

I have a strong desire to emulate this and by the time I'm 40 years old, my goal is to release directly from our loins and influence, 100 preachers into ministry. I'm 37 years old right now. (I'm not talking about just taking people oversees where they receive impartation we've done that already.) We want to be loving fathers who are ready to send laborers/preachers that carry a very high level of anointing in preaching, ministry, character, signs and wonders.

Team counsel

An apostle has a team spirit and gathers with other apostles and elders for counsel at prophetic round tables in various cities, religions and nations. Apostles maintain an attitude that welcomes the wisdom of other apostles from different spheres and locations.

Acts 15:6 And the apostles and elders came together for to consider of this matter.

Signs, Wonders and Perseverance

Many who walk in a true apostolic anointing can even raise the dead! (This is the most spectacular sign and wonder.)

Here's what Paul said,

2 Corinthians 12:12 Truly the signs of an apostle were wrought among you in all patience, in signs, and wonders, and mighty deeds.

Notably, true apostles never give up easily; they persevere in signs, wonders and mighty deeds, not getting disappointed and discouraged. They just keep going. If they pray for one thousand and nobody is healed, then they pray for another thousand! Perseverance!

Humility

An apostle walks in humility; Paul models humility:
Philippians 2:3 *Let* nothing *be done* through strife or vainglory; but in lowliness of mind let each esteem other better than themselves.

1 Corinthians 15:9 For I am the least of the apostles, that am not meet to be called an apostle, because I persecuted the church of God.

Servanthood

1 Corinthians 11:1 Be ye followers of me, even as I also *am* of Christ.

That's a pretty big statement for Paul to make. I've been really challenged by that verse. I've also wondered how that one would look in my life. If I really said to all the people who follow me, "Imitate me," what would that look like? Paul was telling the Corinthians to follow Christ in everything they did; they were to imitate him in living solely for the Glory of God. He urged the Corinthians to have servant's hearts:

1 Corinthians 10:32, 33 Give none offence, neither to the Jews, nor to the Gentiles, nor to the church of God: Even as I please all *men* in all *things,* not seeking mine own profit, but the *profit* of many, that they may be saved.

The passion of Paul's life was to serve Christ and to serve others. That humble commitment of love it is a mark of the apostolic anointing. An attitude of servanthood always seeks "the profit of many that they may be served."

True Revelatory Gifting

This is such a significant gifting and true apostles receive the anointing to preach the gospel through the revelation of Jesus Christ just like Paul did.

Galatians 1:11, 12 But I certify you, brethren, that the gospel which was preached of me is not after man. For I neither received it of man, neither was I taught *it,* but by the revelation of Jesus Christ.

Remember, for quite some time Paul was persecuting the church of God and he wasn't one of the 12 disciples. So in effect, Paul is saying something like this: I didn't get what I got the way you got it! I wasn't with Jesus like you and hanging out with the apostles. I haven't even been with the apostles. I got it in the wilderness.

I was hanging out for months in the Arabian Desert and for months, by revelation, by visions and dreams and angels who knows how it came? I got what I got! Also, Paul emphasized that he saw the Lord just like all the other apostles did. True apostles, most of the time, possess a strong anointing that is revelatory and prophetic. They can actually change their "apostolic hat" to the "prophetic hat," but also step out into ministry with both hats and like Paul, shake entire cities and plant churches with signs and wonders. An accurate revelatory gifting will accompany a true apostle. There is a frequency of heightened supernatural experiences that come with the apostolic. Apostles have visions and dreams, receive the word of the Lord and they experience open heavens.

Character

God wants to raise up apostles with impeccable character who can be completely trusted. His strategic assignments often involve life and death issues that can affect multitudes of people.

So, God is always examining an apostle's character. But God doesn't just do character checks, He has a plan to build character

This plan is often an excruciating process. God repeatedly tests apostles, using trials and tribulations to reveal their real level of character. Apostles-in the- making willingly go through this maturing process because they want to please the Lord and to fulfill His call on their lives. Not only do tribulations help build character, they also produce perseverance and hope. The apostle Paul preached about this:

Romans 5:3-5 And not only *so,* but we glory in tribulations also: knowing that tribulation worketh patience; And patience, experience; and experience, hope: And hope maketh not ashamed; because the love of God is shed abroad in our hearts by the Holy Ghost which is given unto us.

Apostles that patiently allow God to refine their character will be fully equipped and carry a strong authority to bring a message of hope to the world the message of salvation through Jesus Christ! Exceptional character and a good reputation go hand in hand. True apostles who submit to the Father's dealings will receive grace, favor and a good name from Him.

Proverbs 22:1 A *good* name *is* rather to be chosen than great riches, *and* loving favour rather than silver and gold. Favor comes from God and is something more precious than money.

Breaking Out

Like Paul, modern-day apostles' pioneer into new territory; they don't want to build on anyone else's foundation. They boldly enter dangerous places and they live to break uncharted areas wide open with the gospel.

Here is what Paul said,
Romans 15:20, 21 Yea, so have I strived to preach the gospel, not where Christ was named, lest I should build upon another man's foundation: But as it is written, To whom he was not spoken of, they shall see: and they that have not heard shall understand. Apostles actually enjoy the adventure of new frontiers; their hearts are set on a pilgrimage. Apostles, operating in their kingly authority, will always "break out" into new territory and discover new ways of extending the kingdom of God with power.

Jesus also gave me a revelation that until the church understands that the prayer movement (intercession, worship, 24/7 prayer watch of the Lord, the house of prayer) and the evangelism/healing movement go hand in hand, we hinder God from releasing the great harvest.

Prayer and evangelism must be seen as parts of the same movement the apostolic movement which ultimately ends in revival and the great harvest. The tabernacle of David, continual priestly worship, sacrifice and intercession, must return to the church before the harvest is reaped. Around the world, we can see great evidence of God's people building the house of prayer. We're in the midst of a glorious construction project, but we've got a long way to go. After my vision, I realized that the apostle James gives us insights regarding the mystery of the tabernacle of David that can help us. In the midst of revival and great harvest of Jewish and Gentile believers, in Acts 15, James addresses the Jerusalem counsel.

Acts 15:16 After this I will return, and will build again the tabernacle of David, which is fallen down; and I will build again the ruins thereof, and I will set it up:

His interpretation of the great harvest (thousands being added to the church daily with miracles, signs and wonders) was the beginning of the prophetic restoration of the tabernacle of David. I began understanding that the house of prayer being built today was the "forerunner" that would release the great healing revival.

Before I discuss how the tabernacle of David will be restored in our day, let's take a look at how this prayer movement will look during the great harvest. To begin, let's look at this passage, which, I believe, is very prophetic of the days we are in:
Amos 9:11-13 In that day will I raise up the tabernacle of David that is fallen, and close up the breaches thereof; and I will raise up his ruins, and I will build it as in the days of old: That they may possess the remnant of Edom, and of all the heathen, which are called by my name, saith the LORD that doeth this. Behold, the days come, saith the LORD, that the plowman shall overtake the reaper, and the treader of grapes him that soweth seed; and the mountains shall drop sweet wine, and all the hills shall melt.

This tabernacle of David prayer movement, I believe, first triggers a healing revival, then the great end-time harvest. In the books of Acts, we see an example of an apostolic movement marked by continual prayer. First, the Acts outpouring was birthed in 10 days of prayer and waiting on the Holy Spirit. Next, even in the midst of signs and wonders, the apostles upheld this priority of prayer.

Amos 6:4 That lie upon beds of ivory, and stretch themselves upon their couches, and eat the lambs out of the flock, and the calves out of the midst of the stall;

This apostolic prayer movement launched and maintained the healing movement in the early church. Then the healing movement released the great harvest of souls:

Acts 2:47 Praising God, and having favour with all the people. And the Lord added to the church daily such as should be saved.

I believe that the apostolic movement we are entering into will follow some of the same steps of the early church prayer, healing then harvest. We've begun to enter into what's happening in prayer and healing already, but we haven't quite yet begun to enter into what's happening in harvest. But I tell you, its coming! Well, what can we expect God to do in our church, city and region?

God says that He is going to raise up the tabernacles of David which has fallen down the house of prayer days and He will repair its damages and days are coming when the plowman shall overtake the reaper. Now when is this great harvest? It happens in the days that the mountains drip with sweet wine (renewal and refreshing) when the plowman shall over take the reaper. In the sweet wine there is a promise of the days of acceleration. And these days are upon us!

The sowing and reaping time is speeding up! God will do in a day what He used to in six months and in a minute what He used to do in an hour. He's going to do in seconds what He used to do in minutes and when people say, "I found Jesus," they're in the ministry almost right away! Now, thank God for this whole Moses and 40 years! What about the disciples? They were full-fledged apostles in just a few years. You know, I believe in the whole process even if it takes some years to mature in the Lord, but things are changing. God is quickening the pace! Just watch what God is doing with young people today! Within many of them, the maturity and wisdom is well beyond their years. For myself, I am amazed to be teaching and writing books like I am. I'll tell you what. The harvest isn't just the harvest of money and the harvest of healing! It's the harvest of everything else in the kingdom that comes in seed form! The bread that we cast on the waters is coming back to us!

At the same time as this harvest, the healing and prayer movements are emphasized, as well as the restoration of ministry and worship.

I want to discuss several scriptures from the Old and New Testaments that will help to paint a picture of the coming healing revival.

Malachi 4:1, 2 For, behold, the day cometh, that shall burn as an oven; and all the proud, yea, and all that do wickedly, shall be stubble: and the day that cometh shall burn them up, saith the LORD of hosts, that it shall leave them neither root nor branch. But unto you that fear my name shall the Sun of righteousness arise with healing in his wings; and ye shall go forth, and grow up as calves of the stall. In verse one; Malachi begins by sounding a severe warning of a refining fire to come. But in the midst of this cleansing, God pours out His power: "But to you who fear my name, the Sun of Righteousness shall arise with healings in His wings?"

Healing revival comes in His wings. Scripture also tells us that we can find shelter and safety from "deadly pestilence" under the shadow of His wings.

Psalms 91:3 Surely he shall deliver thee from the snare of the fowler, *and* from the noisome pestilence.

Now let's look at the healing blessing of this shadow depicted in the book of Acts.

Acts 5:12 And by the hands of the apostles were many signs and wonders wrought among the people; (and they were all with one accord in Solomon's porch.

Notice that the signs and wonders were released "through the hands of the apostles." But it wasn't just their hands look at this:

Acts 5:15, 16 Insomuch that they brought forth the sick into the streets, and laid *them* on beds and couches, that at the least the shadow of Peter passing by might overshadow some of them. There came also a multitude *out* of the cities round about unto Jerusalem, bringing sick folks, and them which were vexed with unclean spirits: and they were healed every one.

The very presence of the apostles brought healing! Did you know that there is a distinction between the hands of the apostles and the presence of the apostles? We can be encourage by these scriptures a time is coming when true modern-day apostles will carry a new dimension of healing manifested by God, through their very presence. As well, when that kind of presence is carried into a room or building, the sick are healed in that atmosphere, or resident anointing because of the intensity of God's manifest presence in that place.

It's all about the Son of Righteousness saying, "I want that whole city to come under the shadow of my healing wings and when it happens, it's a healing atmosphere where even as people are lying on beds and couches in the streets, they are healed. Not because of the anointing that is on the hands of the apostles, but because of the anointing that is on the presence of the apostles." Not only does the Lord want to release healing through the anointing on the lives of individuals, He also wants to dig wells of healing in cities. Today, all over the world, He is establishing healing rooms, safe places where people can go to receive deep ministry. As well, the John G. Lake anointing and resident anointing is being released, along with an emphasis on the restoration of the Voice of Healing Movement. The church is about to see a healing revival greater than the healing revivals of the 1940's, 50's and 60's. The healing signs are already here and it will usher us into the Second Coming. One of the last moves of God will be a healing revival!

You can read a lot more about the coming revival in one of my other books Waves of Revival.

Now, when will this healing revival come? I believe we will see this great move of the Spirit when God builds on the sure foundation, described by the apostle Paul, in this scripture:
Ephesians 2:19-22 Now therefore ye are no more strangers and foreigners, but fellowcitizens with the saints, and of the household of God; And are built upon the foundation of the apostles and prophets, Jesus Christ himself being the chief corner *stone;* In whom all the building fitly framed

together growth unto an holy temple in the Lord: In whom ye also are builded together for an habitation of God through the Spirit. This Church's foundation is to be the apostles and prophets; Jesus Christ Himself is the chief cornerstone. God will continue building His church by raising up apostles and prophets and anointing them to help His body mature.

Repentance from sin and tradition is vital in this process. That's why John the Baptist and the prophet Elijah had ministries that called the people to major repentance. God will pour out a spirit of repentance through these foundational ministries many people, as a result, will experience severe distress and truly repent over their sinful condition. I believe that holiness and the conviction of sin will reside in the church once again and whole cities will cry out in repentance. The Lord will respond to this godly sorrow and true brokenness with gifts of cleansing, forgiveness, redemption and restoration in the lives of His children.

2 Chronicles 7:14, 15 If my people, which are called by my name, shall humble themselves, and pray, and seek my face, and turn from their wicked ways; then will I hear from

heaven, and will forgive their sin, and will heal their land. Now mine eyes shall be open, and mine ears attent unto the prayer *that is made* in this place.

Such deep healing is a vital part of the healing revival. As a result of this repentance, God will restore an anointing for evangelism, miracles, signs and wonders to the church and specifically, to his apostles and prophets. Now, I want to talk about forerunners. God sends apostles and prophets with a forerunner anointing, who work ahead of time (often behind the scenes), to "prepare the way," so that God's plans and purposes may begin. They prepare the church for the new things God wants to do. Both John and Elijah were forerunners; I believe this anointing is at work in our day. The prophet Isaiah and Zachariah (John's father) both prophesied about John's forerunner anointing, saying,
Isaiah 40:3 The voice of him that crieth in the wilderness, Prepare ye the way of the LORD, make straight in the desert a highway for our God.

After John launched into ministry with his message of repentance, he described Himself as the voice of one crying in the wilderness:

Matthew 3:1-3 In those days came John the Baptist, preaching in the wilderness of Judaea, And saying, Repent ye: for the kingdom of heaven is at hand. For this is he that was spoken of by the prophet Esaias, saying, The voice of one crying in the wilderness, Prepare ye the way of the Lord, make his paths straight.

He was actually quoting Isaiah the prophet's words about the coming forerunner. John himself was that forerunner, one preparing the ground for the appearance and ministry of Jesus Christ. In Malachi 4, the prophet speaks of the Son of Righteousness rising with healing in His wings; he also announces the coming of,
Malachi 4:5 Behold, I will send you Elijah the prophet before the coming of the great and dreadful day of the LORD: Healing and the Elijah anointing seem to go hand in hand. However, the religious leaders did not realize that the spirit of Elijah had rested on John the Baptist.

Many Pharisees and Sadducees wouldn't receive Jesus Christ as Messiah because they knew Malachi 4, that Elijah the prophet must come first to prepare the way of the Lord. The

disciples couldn't understand the Pharisees' arguments so they:
Matthew 17:10 And his disciples asked him, saying, Why then say the scribes that Elias must first come?

Jesus answered something like this, "Well if you can receive it guys, Elijah has come already." Yes, in those days, people were wondering where Elijah was, waiting for the dude to show up and walk around Israel again. They didn't understand that Elijah had already come and gone; they missed it because they really didn't think he would come in the form of John the Baptist (who came in the spirit and power of Elijah.) What about that forerunner anointing today? I believe it is already here! It's already happening.

The anointing of Elijah is coming upon the church (the lampstand), Jew and Gentile alike. It will shake entire cities and nations; they will demonstrate the kind of power Moses and Elijah demonstrated. That is what the end time lampstands are going to do! I hope the picture I've painted in this section gives you clear idea of what the coming healing revival will look like.

We're going to jump tracks for a little bit! We are living in the days spoken of in Acts chapters 5 and 13 and Amos 9 and Malachi 4. The great harvest is coming. There is a little sweet wine there too! To build the character of the apostolic, promotions and apostolic authority are coming from the Lord that will change current levels of authority, identity and position. Paul talks about the apostles having their spheres of influence, government and authority, but did you know that God could give us more?

Eventually he went about preaching with Barnabas. The scriptures repeat several times (Acts 11:30, Acts 12:25, Acts 13:1, 2) that it was always Barnabas and Saul; Barnabas leading the way. As they ministered to the Lord and fasted, the Holy Spirit said, "Now separate to Me Barnabas and Saul for the work to which I have called them."

Acts 13:2 As they ministered to the Lord, and fasted, the Holy Ghost said, Separate me Barnabas and Saul for the work whereunto I have called them.

But when the prophets and teachers laid hands on them there was ordination and a transfer of anointing. They were sent out by the Holy Ghost.

Acts 13:3 And when they had fasted and prayed, and laid *their* hands on them, they sent *them* away.

The next thing we see is Saul being renamed Paul and then watch it's the popcorn release! From that day forward it would never be Barnabas as the first man and Saul as the second man.

Acts 13:13 Now when Paul and his company loosed from Paphos, they came to Perga in Pamphylia: and John departing from them returned to Jerusalem. One service and an anointing were transferred and it became Paul and Barnabas.

This is an example of what I believe God wants to do today. There can be an anointing release and instantly we are changed and we go from being "Barnabas and Saul" to "Paul and Barnabas." Do you see the change in authority here? Apostle means sent one and a messenger. But it's by the will of God and not man. There are too many people today that don't even move in the signs of an apostle, but just because they are good at gathering crowds and people, they're called an apostle. There are true signs that come with the apostolic. I believe the first true sign is that we will know them by their fruit and not when they say "I'm an apostle."

The people who are true apostles don't even want to be called an apostle. "Just receive me as a father or an apostolic figure; if I am an apostle, God knows. That's good enough for me. If it's real, the anointing will be there whether I say I have it or not."

A whole new government is coming to the church. It's apostolic. Coming to a close, are the days where the church is top-heavy with status/regard over names, positions and government. No longer will the church be run by a board figure heads with authority controlling the pastor and everything else that happens. Likewise, no longer will the church be run by the pastor, with the elders and deacons. I've been around the world and visited many great churches, but most of them are either run by the pastor, or it's the other way where the board is the top and you have to be careful to keep the board happy.

APOSTOLIC BREAKTHROUGH

This new structure will encompass apostles, prophets, pastors, teachers, evangelists and team ministries running churches. They will yield to one another and recognize each other after the spirit and have freedom to operate in their different anointing. Competition will not exist; friendship, relationship and a team spirit will be the order of the day. Senior pastors will trust their senior prophet, senior teacher and apostolic authority, based on their solid relationship. There will be camaraderie in what God is doing. Local churches will exist, but the face and the government of the local church will change. I see this new face or new structure, being established in apostolic centers. I know these changes won't come easily because it's a new thing God is doing. There isn't even much language for this new movement, and so, at this stage most people are walking cautiously into it. I'm encouraged to realize that so many Christians are ready to take part in the new things God has purposed to accomplish in these last days.

Even though we lack many clear details, yet, let's say "Yes!" to a move of God in our churches, cities, region and nation. Let's commit ourselves to this new apostolic move: "God, I am ready to pay the price. Here I am,

Lord, send me. This is what I want. From this day forward I want to dedicate myself wholeheartedly in this present move of God. This is what I am going to live for and what I am going to contend for." Right now, God's people are hungry for spiritual gifts, mantles, anointing and commissioning. It's not going to be a Barnabas and Saul commissioning; it's going to be an instant Paul commissioning.

We're ready for a change of identity, position, government, influence and promotion, to come from the Lord. I believe God is releasing promotions for some of you. Some of you will be changing garments; you're not going to be wearing the same thing. It's not going to fit the same. God is a rewarder of those who diligently seek him. I say, it's a reward time!

Apostolic Breakthrough Decrees

There are decrees and then there are apostolic decrees. There is a higher realm of authority coming through apostolic breakthrough. APOSTOLIC declarations, that are commissioned in heaven and sent by God, have tremendous authority to bring about His justice. The Lord will release significant breakthroughs when we declare decree and proclaim His will and His word. An apostolic declaration is a powerful weapon that shatters destructive plans of the enemy! It's even like a pre-emptive strike!

God began speaking to me about apostolic declarations. He highlighted this key scripture, Isaiah 61:2 To proclaim the acceptable year of the LORD, and the day of vengeance of our God; to comfort all that mourn;

He revealed mandates for the coming years and beyond is: to declare, decree and proclaim the acceptable year of the Lord, the

year of the Lord's favor or Jubilee. He is anointing us to carry out this mandate! When we make a decree like Moses and the prophet Isaiah, it's like we're saying,
Deuteronomy 32:1 Give ear, O ye heavens, and I will speak; and hear, O earth, the words of my mouth.

Isaiah 1:2 Hear, O heavens, and give ear, O earth: for the LORD hath spoken, I have nourished and brought up children, and they have rebelled against me.

Did you know that Jubilee means total deliverance for us, cancellation of debts for each of us and our family and liberation from any kind of a bondage, taskmaster or oppression over our lives? In the anointing, we can proclaim "Jubilee!" and set into motion, like the laws of gravity, a power or a force of power that causes everything in our lives to begin to come into divine order.

Now, that's an anointing! We don't have to wait for the year of Jubilee! When God's word is declared, the angels of heaven act upon that decree and a supernatural endowment of power comes into our lives that we never had before. There's more! When the Spirit of the

Lord God is upon us to proclaim "Favor!" Everything around us will begin to change because of the favor of God. One moment we don't have this power, and then in the next moment, under the anointing, we can proclaim, "Favor, favor, favor!" Suddenly, a download of favor comes that was lacking two minutes before, like a tangible 'coat of many colors,' dropping out of heaven as an anointing. We will see the results! Did you know that the same word for 'grace' is 'favor' and both words can be used in the same way? How many of us would just love a spirit of grace to come upon us today? God not only wants to give us favor, He wants to release the spirit of grace upon us, through a supernatural endowment of power.

It seems like everyone is trying to get favor, but there are principles involved that release favor upon our lives. First of all, God is a rewarder of those who diligently seek Him (Hebrews 11:6). God loves everyone the same, but the one who loves and seeks Him the most, is the one He will favor the most. God loves the wickedest, vilest sinner just as much as He loves us, but more of His favor is released to the one who deeply loves Him, who hungers and thirsts for Him. When we fail

to seek God passionately, our favor level might not be the same as other believers who are pursing the Lord with all their heart. Jesus said to,
Matthew 7:7 Ask, and it shall be given you; seek, and ye shall find; knock, and it shall be opened unto you:

We can actually grow in favor by obedience and by diligently seeking Him. When we think about getting the favor of God, so often we think it's a process of getting into the favor. But levels of favor grow.

Jesus grew in favor with both God and men. When our favor with God grows, our favor with man grows.

Luke 2:52 And Jesus increased in wisdom and stature, and in favour with God and man.

King David's life of devotion to the Lord attracted the heart and favor of God; Even though at times there were some areas of his life that were quite messy. It was like God looked at David and said, "But this guy has a heart of passion for Me!" When David became captain over about 400 discontented men, the favor of God became evident and this favor grew until the people made him King over Judah and all of Israel.

1 Samuel 22:2 And every one *that was* in distress, and every one that *was* in debt, and every one *that was* discontented, gathered themselves unto him; and he became a captain over them: and there were with him about four hundred men.

1 Samuel 2:4 The bows of the mighty men *are* broken, and they that stumbled are girded with strength.

So, growing in favor with God, hinges on our intense pursuit of Him. When God sees our love for Him and our determination to chase after Him with all our heart, He not only releases favor over our lives, He releases an anointing to proclaim "Favor!" You know, there's more than Jubilee and favor coming! Our day of vindication is coming, too! Now, let's go back in Isaiah to,
Isaiah 61:2 To proclaim the acceptable year of the LORD, and the day of vengeance of our God; to comfort all that mourn;

The second part of that verse is to declare and decree the day of the vengeance of our

God. He will release an anointing upon us so that we can actually call court into session and call heaven to be our witness, when there is injustice. It's an anointing to declare God's vindication (Definition vindication: defending against criticism or censure [Webster's Dictionary]).

We can access the heavenly court system where the Holy Ghost presides as our advocate and counselor in matters concerning our lives, destiny, inheritance and death. How many of us would like God to take up our cause right now? There are circumstances in our lives sickness, disease, death, poverty, bondage, oppression, false accusations that we know are not God's will for us. Yes, we can think of all kinds of injustice, but the Spirit of the Lord is upon us to declare vindication. We know the scripture where God says "Vengeance is Mine, I will repay," says the Lord, but He has invited us, as saints of God, into a place of power of the decree.

Hebrews 10:30 For we know him that hath said, Vengeance *belongeth* unto me, I will recompense, saith the Lord. And again, The Lord shall judge his people.

We can actually approach the heavenly court system; not only to gain justice on our behalf, but also to petition God for divine judgment against our enemies. God will plead the cause of His people, but we have to learn how to ascend the courts of heaven. As children of God we have a right to see injustice removed and it will be removed when we declare and proclaim God's word, His truth. God's word prevails and disarms injustice!

Now, let's examine some background scriptures so we can more fully understand how our decrees disarm injustice in the heavenly realm. The heavenly court system is known by other names in scripture:
a) Divine council?
Psalms 82:1
b) Counsel of El (God)?
Job 15:8
c) The council of Yahweh?
Jeremiah 23:18
d) Council of the holy ones?
Psalms 89:7

I'd like to define divine 'council,' and divine counsel. When a group meets together like an administrative, advisory or legislative body for discussion and advice, we call this grouping, a

council. So, when the heavenly court is in session, the members of the court form a body called the divine council. But, when these members of the divine council listen to the Lord's message and engage in discussion, the members are hearing God's advice and wisdom and His divine counsel. Below, I will list some of the members of the divine council:
a) God
b) The Hosts of heaven also called the stars of heaven: "They fought from the heavens; The stars from their courses fought against Sisera" Judges 5:20 (The hosts of heaven include: the angels: the Cherubim and the Seraphim, Michael, the archangel, who is the leader of angels in battle and the archangel over the nation of Israel and Gabrielle, who brings interpretation of divine revelation concerning times and season of the church.)
c) The cloud of witnesses: the apostles, prophets and saints of old
d) The prophets that are alive on the earth and believers
e) The twelve disciples who judge the nation of Israel
f) The 24 elders
g) Devils

The divine counsel of God is described differently in several places in scripture. The heavenly courts can be found on earth or in heaven and both the counsel and council of God are always linked to the dwelling place of God. It can happen in the mountain it can happen in the temple setting:
a) The mound of the congregation:
Isaiah 14:13
b) The holy mountain of God:
Ezekiel 28:14
c) An earthly picture linked to the tent or Tabernacle of God:
Isaiah 33:20

When he comes before the throne in the spirit, the apostle John sees God, sitting on the throne, like jasper stone and sardius in appearance. He sees a beautiful scene of worship.

Revelations 4:1-11 After this I looked, and, behold, a door *was* opened in heaven: and the first voice which I heard *was* as it were of a trumpet talking with me; which said, Come up hither, and I will shew thee things which must be hereafter. And immediately I was in the spirit: and, behold, a throne was set in heaven, and *one* sat on the throne. And he that sat was to look upon like a jasper and a sardine stone: and *there was* a rainbow round about the throne, in sight like unto an emerald. And round about the throne *were* four and twenty seats: and upon the seats I saw four and twenty elders sitting, clothed in white raiment; and they had on their heads crowns of gold. And out of the throne proceeded lightnings and thunderings and voices: and *there were* seven lamps of fire burning before the throne, which are the seven Spirits of God. And before the throne *there was* a sea of glass like unto crystal: and in the midst of the throne, and round about the throne, *were* four beasts full of eyes before and behind. And the first beast *was* like a lion, and the second beast like a calf, and the third beast had a face as a man, and the fourth beast *was* like a flying eagle. And the four beasts had each of them six wings about *him;* and *they were* full of eyes within: and they rest not day and night, saying, Holy, holy, holy, Lord God Almighty, which was, and is, and is to come. And when those beasts give glory and honour and thanks to him that sat on the throne, who liveth for ever and ever, The four and twenty elders fall down before him that sat on the throne, and worship him that liveth for ever and ever, and cast their crowns before the throne, saying, Thou art worthy, O Lord, to receive glory and honour and power: for thou hast created all things, and for thy pleasure they are and were created.

Later, in the book of Revelation chapters five through eight, although the setting remains the same the very throne of God, the scene changes to a courtroom that releases judgment.

As Christians, we often have a mental picture of two distinct places in heaven: one, the throne room where the saints worship and two, the courtroom of God where judgments are made. However, in the book of Revelation, it appears that both worship and judgment happen in the same place, just at different times. In the throne room John sees and refers to each member of the Trinity. Firstly, he identifies God as "One sitting on the throne." (Revelation 5) as the Lion of the Tribe of Judah, the great overcomer. There it is the Trinity: Father, Son and Holy Ghost, in the throne room! The prophet, Daniel, gives one of the best descriptions of the throne room to be found in scripture; both the Ancient of Days and the Son of Man are seen together in their governmental authority:

Daniel 7:9, 10 I beheld till the thrones were cast down, and the Ancient of days did sit, whose garment *was* white as snow, and the hair of his head like the pure wool: his throne *was like* the fiery flame, *and* his wheels *as* burning fire. A fiery stream issued and came forth from before him: thousand thousands ministered unto him, and ten thousand times ten thousand stood before him: the judgment was set, and the books were opened.

In the above passage, Daniel identifies the Ancient of Days as the one presiding over judgment and the Son of Man, Jesus Christ, receiving His glorious kingdom. Both Daniel and John describe the presence of the Lamb of God. Revelation 4 and Ezekiel 1 and 10 describe the throne, but in two different ways.

The Apostle John refers to a throne on the ground, on the sea of glass like crystal. On the other hand, in his vision, Ezekiel looks up to the throne through the firmament. He sees the throne, moving on wheels within the wheels and covered in eyes. Again, both prophetic books speak of four living creatures, but in different ways. Although Revelation doesn't speak of a throne with wheels, Ezekiel describes four living creatures that actually create a celestial chariot for the throne to ride on.

That's why the throne has wheels, it moves. Did you know the throne of God rides on a chariot with wheels and that the four living creatures actually form part of the chariot that carries the throne? It's a prophetic picture of the Levitical priests who carried the Ark of the Covenant, which was a symbol and actual sign of God's presence. Where the ark went, so did the presence of God.

1 Chronicles 15:2 Then David said, None ought to carry the ark of God but the Levites: for them hath the LORD chosen to carry the ark of God, and to minister unto him for ever. Whenever we talk about the throne room we should picture it like the tabernacle of Moses (Exodus Chapter 35 to 38) and the temple of Solomon (1 Kings Chapter 6 to 8) all the tabernacle imagery. We can think of every reference to the throne of God as a reference to the ark of God as well both symbolize the presence of God, the place where God was. Also, both the ark and the throne moved as God's presence moved.

The divine council room, also called the heavenly court, is situated in the Throne Room. Remember, it's a place where judgments are decided upon, but it also functions as a throne room of worship. Let's keep in mind that the devil can come before the throne of judgment, bringing accusations against believers, but he doesn't have access to the throne room of worship. One descriptive scene of demonic involvement in the council room is found in,

1 Kings 22:19-23 And he said, Hear thou therefore the word of the LORD: I saw the LORD sitting on his throne, and all the host of heaven standing by him on his right hand and on his left. And the LORD said, Who shall persuade Ahab, that he may go up and fall at Ramothgilead? And one said on this manner, and another said on that manner. And there came forth a spirit, and stood before the LORD, and said, I will persuade him. And the LORD said unto him, Wherewith? And he said, I will go forth, and I will be a lying spirit in the mouth of all his prophets. And he said, Thou shalt persuade *him,* and prevail also: go forth, and do so. Now therefore, behold, the LORD hath put a lying spirit in the mouth of all these thy prophets, and the LORD hath spoken evil concerning thee. This portion of

scripture gives us a picture of a court session going on in heaven. Micah, the prophet, begins by describing the Lord sitting on His throne, surrounded by the host of heaven. We read that an evil spirit answers the Lord's question. "Who will persuade Ahab to go up, that he may fall at Ramoth Gilead?" The demon comes forward, replying: "I will persuade him. I will go out and be a lying spirit in the mouth of his prophets." Then the Lord gives permission to the evil spirit: "You shall persuade him and also prevail. Go out and do it." So, even evil spirits, at times, can be a part of the divine council of heaven to accomplish God's will! But evil spirits don't have the last say! We have a part in judgment against our adversary the devil, who is constantly battling against prosperity coming into our lives.

Although we need God to bring judgment, He invites us to be involved in the divine counsel concerning our life and death, our fate and inheritance. The past biblical and spiritual leaders, had access to the divine council room. Joshua, one such leader, was seen by Zechariah standing before the Lord in the heavenly courts. After satan's unsuccessful attempt to oppose Joshua and after his filthy garments were replaced by rich robes, here's what the Lord said to him.

Zechariah 3:7 Thus saith the LORD of hosts; If thou wilt walk in my ways, and if thou wilt keep my charge, then thou shalt also judge my house, and shalt also keep my courts, and I will give thee places to walk among these that stand by. Joshua was given access to walk among heavens council. Also, we can see, after examining the life of the prophet, Jeremiah, that he was a godly, righteous, man of God who stood in the counsel of the Lord and then pronounced God's judgments.

In the following verses, even though God is asking the question: "For who has stood in the counsel of the Lord and has perceived and heard His word?" We can safely identify Jeremiah as one who stood in the counsel of the Lord while God's judgments were pronounced on the wicked:
Jeremiah 23:18-20 For who hath stood in the counsel of the LORD, and hath perceived and heard his word? who hath marked his word, and heard *it?* Behold, a whirlwind of the LORD is gone forth in fury, even a grievous whirlwind: it shall fall grievously upon the head of the wicked. The anger of the LORD shall

not return, until he have executed, and till he have performed the thoughts of his heart: in the latter days ye shall consider it perfectly.

Angels freely execute the judgments of God echoed in heaven after we decree what God has spoken to us on the earth.

After a decision or judgment is made in heaven, a member of the divine council either serves as a divine messenger to announce the decision of the council or an angel will come to execute the divine judgment. King David writes prophetically about the ministry of angels:

Psalms 103:19-21 The LORD hath prepared his throne in the heavens; and his kingdom ruleth over all. Bless the LORD, ye his angels, that excel in strength, that do his commandments, hearkening unto the voice of his word. Bless ye the LORD, all *ye* his hosts; *ye* ministers of his, that do his pleasure.

Failing to accept our responsibility to make the decrees that God has spoken hinders angels from intervening in our lives. We are called to make heavenly decrees or kingly judgments as His ambassadors. However, God wants us to stop making unrighteous judgments, to stop looking at situations through human eyes.

Until we make righteous judgments and decrees about situations, God cannot release the true breakthroughs we desire! Here's what the Lord said about His people's judgments:
Psalms 82:1 A Psalm of Asaph. God standeth in the congregation of the mighty; he judgeth among the gods.

God is standing in the congregations of the earth, judging among the mighty ones or little "g"----gods, you and me. The word here for mighty is also judges, rulers or sons of God. So, He's standing in the middle of the leaders, apostles, prophets and saints on the earth, ones like us, who are entrusted with power to make prophetic decrees and proclamation. He's judging our judgments, our proclamations, to set the captives free; He's judging our mercy to the widow and to the poor. He asks, "How long will you judge unjustly and show partiality to the wicked?" It's like He's saying, "Haven't I made you my judges? Have I not made you sons of God in the earth?

I've given you power through the prophetic decree. Life and death are in the power of the tongue to announce My word and the angels heed to the voice of your word in bringing about My divine judgment and justice." God commands the mighty ones in verse three: "Defend the poor and the fatherless. Do justice to the afflicted and needy." And then in verse six, God says, "You are judges and all of you are children of the Most High, you shall still die like men and fall like one of his princes." Judges refers to the supreme judges here on the earth as you and me. Clearly, God is commanding us to bring forth justice on behalf of the poor and the fatherless. We are called, with great responsibility and power, to make judgments through the prophetic decree against the enemy.

Asaph concludes his Psalm by pleading with God:
Psalms 82:8 Arise, O God, judge the earth: for thou shalt inherit all nations. He invites God to bring His judgment back into the earth because we are failing to bring forth justice.

But God command us, through the prophetic decree, to execute His divine judgment and justice. Although we are called the mighty ones, and God made us judges, it's God, the King, who rules! He prepared a way and a place, a heavenly courtroom and a functioning heavenly court administration or system, where His will is to be executed. But, to participate in God's heavenly court system, to activate His saving, healing, delivering power on behalf of those who are bound and oppressed, it takes a prophetic decree by us, the mighty ones.

Several scriptures in the book of Job reveal the power of the prophetic decree, expressed through Job's friend, Eliphaz:
Job 22:27-29 Thou shalt make thy prayer unto him, and he shall hear thee, and thou shalt pay thy vows. Thou shalt also decree a thing, and it shall be established unto thee: and the light shall shine upon thy ways. When *men* are cast down, then thou shalt say, *There is* lifting up; and he shall save the humble person.

Job's friend understood the heart of God when he said, "You will decree a thing and it will be established" and "When they cast you down and you declare." This scripture gives us the key to victory declaring God's will! Our breakthroughs are released when we obediently declare God's will; our words activate angels to heed the voice of His word. So, when we declare God's will that prosperity and healing or exaltation will come and victory or favor will come we actually release God to save the humble. Remember, God shall plead the cause of His people.

As stewards and members of the heavenly court or divine council, when we declare and sing in faith, "Exaltation will come," then He will come and save the humble person. He will deliver the one, even the one who is not innocent, at our decree.

Believers who place great value on what God values bring great delight to Him. Listen! He gave us the opportunity to be channels that release His saving, healing and delivering power, when we declare His word and His will. This is no small thing in His sight! But, today if we fail to proclaim liberty to the captives and recovery of sight to the blind, then their destiny is jeopardized, robbed and plundered. Isaiah expresses God's heart when he writes:
Isaiah 42:22 But this *is* a people robbed and spoiled; *they are* all of them snared in holes, and they are hid in prison houses: they are for

a prey, and none delivereth; for a spoil, and none saith, Restore.

You know what? Now days, we're not doing a very good job speaking healing words to the sick, proclaiming liberty to the captives or decreeing freedom for the prisoners. (Our destiny is adversely affected, too, when we neglect to decree God's word and His will.) That's why God was judging the mighty ones in Psalms 82; He was saying, "You're not taking care of the poor, the needy and the afflicted. You're not making decrees of justice." There are believers in the church today, caught in addiction and bondage, hidden in prison houses. There's so much defeat! If we're honest, we'll admit that there are times when our back is up against the wall. We think, "Hey, I know who's going to win in the end, but I'm losing right now and I don't know what's going on!" Yet, when we start to rise up in authority, making declarations to set captives free, we're still not seeing the victory we're contending for. Our problem is not in the words we decree, but in the faith behind them. We often don't really believe that there really is authority and power in our words.

God is actually hindered from saving the humble and wreaking vengeance on the enemy when we don't understand the power in the declarations: "Exaltation will come," and "Decree a thing and it will be established" (Job 22:28, 29). We must learn how to approach the heavenly courtroom and utilize the provision God made for us there in that setting. Remember, the angels either announce or execute the decisions made in the heavenly court. These heavenly ministries carry out our earthly prophetic decrees which line up with the truth of God's word and His will. So, God wants to save and bring restoration to the humble! I believe that His power to restore is set into motion when we declare: "Restore!" "Restore!" Then the angels in heaven are released to execute this righteous and just decree!

We're in a battle right now! We're being prevailed against! So often our back is up against the wall and we're getting the short end of the stick. Some of us are losing in the fight against sin and sickness, disease and death. We're contending for prosperity and fulfillment of the prophetic word in our lives. The fight is on for our kids to know Jesus. We're fighting for that mortgage that land, that property. This war has raged for centuries! The prophet, Daniel saw this war we would face today: "I was watching; and the same horn was making war against the saints and prevailing against them" (Daniel 7:21). This was is with the antichrist or the anit-anointing spirit. It reminds us of the battle outlined in Daniel 10 about the Prince of Persia opposing Michael the archangel for 21 days. As the enemy opposed Daniel, the anti anointing and anti-christ spirits oppose our every destiny and inheritance in God UNTIL....

Daniel 7:22 Until the Ancient of days came, and judgment was given to the saints of the most High; and the time came that the saints possessed the kingdom.

When the Ancient of Days comes to execute judgment on our behalf, we will have justice in our lives. Today could be the day! Right now, we could ascend the courts of heaven, approach the Ancient of Days, Judge and present our case! We could begin to act as sons of God on the earth with the power of apostolic declaration in our mouth! As we say "Exaltation will come!" We release God to save the humble and to deliver those who are bound. When we say, "Restore!" we release

God's 'repairer of the breach' anointing (Isaiah 58:12) which will cause everything in our lives that is lost and broken to be restored not just double, not just five times, but seven times the thief must repay God's people. Restoration will happen when we declare, "Restore!" "Restore!" "Exaltation will come!"

Before we begin to approach the heavenly courts, I want you to think about every case that you have right now, and every area of your life that you are waiting for a breakthrough. It could be that the Devil is keeping you from receiving your inheritance and stepping into your destiny. Or your difficulty might be concerning your health; he is bringing sickness and disease by stealing, killing and destroying. Any areas of your life right now where you know there is injustice and you've tried to battle it through yourself think about your case. Maybe you're trying to defend yourself by bringing vengeance by yourself. You need God to plead your cause. When we petition the Ancient of Days in just a moment with our case, the angels are going to heed to the voice of His word spoken by us, the saints. Remember, whenever a decision is made, a member of the divine counsel either serves as a messenger to announce the decision of the counsel, or an angel will come to execute the divine judgment, so that the justice of God can come.

The Old Testament Church was entrusted by God to bring about judgments in their own courts in five matters: life, death, destiny, kingship or inheritance. (You know they had their own courts. Remember when they took Jesus before Pontius Pilate? There were certain boundaries to the courts that the Pharisees, Sadducess and Jews had and so they turned Jesus over to the Romans or how they wanted to stone the woman who was caught in adultery.) Now if you can think of any area of your life right now that you are not living in the fullness of the promise and word of God in these five areas, you have a right today to ascend the courts of heaven and petition the Ancient of Days to come and pronounce judgment in your favor. I've been in meetings when the Lord gave us permission to make decrees resulting in numerous testimonies coming out after. Supernaturally several people had thousands of dollars appear in their bank account right after the service!

God is inviting you to approach His throne to present your case right now. We can petition God together for His judgment and make apostolic declarations and decrees. Remind God of the prophetic promises you received and then name each injustice. Now listen, God is also entrusting us today to begin proclaiming liberty to the captives and the opening of the prison to those who are bound. We can say "Restore!" and "Exaltation will come!" We can begin to bring justice and mercy for the poor and needy, the afflicted and the widow, with the word of God in our mouths. He gave us authority to set the captives free, in Jesus' Mighty name! Now pray with me to execute judgment on earth and to proclaim God's favor in our lives:

God, today, we are petitioning the court of heaven and we are petitioning you, the one who is faithful and just, the one who is true!

The Holy ones today are approaching the courtroom in heaven where judgment is made; divine judgment for divine justice on behalf of the bound and the afflicted and the oppressed. Thank you, Lord, that today we can stand in the council of heaven as prophetic voices, as mighty ones and judges and rulers on this earth with dominion to make the decree. Today, Ancient of Days, with all respect we come before your throne and we make petitions and we make requests. God, together we are petitioning the council members in heaven right now, requesting that the host of heaven begin to hear, with You, the Ancient of Days upon Your throne, concerning where we need Your divine judgment and Your vindication to come. You are the God who rolls back the reproach. You are the God who pleads the cause of your people, the God who pronounces judgment and favor over the saints of the Most High. We petition You today in intercession and we present our cases. Hear them, Please God!

Let the courts of heaven be open right now and let the session come into place right now. We pray that you would come into our homes and congregations into the midst of the might ones. God we are going to make a decree: Exaltation will come! Restore! Restore! Restore! God we loose it in heaven. Restore! Restore! Restore! Divine order coming now. In every area where there has been stealing and killing and destroying we speak the word of the Lord. We say over that loss, Restore! Devil, give it all back! The thief and the liar give it all back! God, we believe You will restore and we claim it! God, we ask for it! We declare it! God, we proclaim the day of your vengeance. We proclaim that this is the year of Your favor! This is the year of the Lord's favor! This is the year! This is our acceptable year, liberation and Jubilee! Lord, I say it over the people today: Favor! Favor! Favor! Divine Favor! I proclaim and I decree: Favor! Favor! Favor! The vengeance of God! The vengeance of God! How I can feel the Glory!

Now, Lord let the angelic hosts who execute your judgment go forth. Let the warring angels act to defeat the enemy and restore our kingly destiny. Let them overcome in the spirit-world, in Jesus name! And let the angelic hosts overcome every demonic power or stronghold and every assignment that is aimed against our inheritances! We throw it down! We take authority concerning our kingship over every power that resists. We know O god, that You must come and make a judgment in favor of the saints; that's what we need right now. We thank you, Lord, today for the victory!

Great Grace

There is a season of Great Grace we are entering into. God is imparting and releasing supernatural grace to His people in this hour to empower them to live an overcoming Christian life! He wants us to understand that He has a higher level of empowering grace available for His children-called great grace- which He is releasing to equip them with His supernatural power for the coming healing revival.

Acts 4:33 And with great power gave the apostles witness of the resurrection of the Lord Jesus: and great grace was upon them all.

Great grace comes as a sovereign anointing from the Holy Spirit, which comes upon believers to enable them to do impossible feats by the spirit of grace.

This supernatural grace includes grace, favor and great grace; also know as "grace, grace."

Zechariah 4:7 Who *art* thou, O great mountain? before Zerubbabel *thou shalt become* a plain: and he shall bring forth the headstone *thereof with* shoutings, *crying,* Grace, grace unto it.

Grace and favor is not only an anointing that can come as tangible presence upon our lives; it can be imparted and transferred as well. The Greek word for grace in the New Testament is the same word for favor. Grace is also the unmerited favor of God; but it's more than that. The grace of God is the favor and kindness that He gives without regard to the worth or merit of the one who receives it, in spite of what that same person deserves. Favor happens when God turns to us and he is pleased with us, I believe it's possible for God to give us favor even if we haven't fasted and prayed enough or we haven't given enough.

I believe that this is the year of the Lord's favor and I'm standing in faith for this! (Isaiah 61:2). The favor of God brings the blessing of the Lord and everything we need in the natural to do what God has called us to do. At times, we must pass through testing before we come into this favor. However, I am saying that this is the year of the Lord's favor.

God is releasing an anointing of His Spirit to bring us into the acceptable year, a place of liberty and release , just like the year of Jubilee in Scripture, Jubilee is the cancellation of all debt, the release of all our property and the release of all slaves (referring to all the bondage in our lives.) Jubilee brings the return of our sons and daughters and the release of our investments. God released all these things in the time of Jubilee!

It is possible, under the anointing of God's Spirit, for us to prophesy, proclaim and decree favor and Jubilee then everything that comes in Jubilee will come into our lives the moment we speak the word. It can happen that fast!

According to Scripture, Jesus increased in favor: "And Jesus increased in wisdom and stature and in favor with God and man." The Bible also tells us about the child, Samuel and how he grew in favor with the Lord and also with man.

APOSTOLIC BREAKTHROUGH

1 Samuel 2:26 And the child Samuel grew on, and was in favour both with the LORD, and also with men.

I want to say that it's time to grow in the favor of the Lord- both with God and man just like Samuel did. But we have to increase in favor with God first, though and then we'll increase in favor with man.

More and more believers are going to come into the anointing that brings the favor of God to the point that He's going to break the spirit of poverty and lack and He's going to release His grace. So, the question is how to obtain the favor of God? The answer is the anointing.

Jesus was anointed with two anointings:
Acts 10:38 How God anointed Jesus of Nazareth with the Holy Ghost and with power: who went about doing good, and healing all that were oppressed of the devil; for God was with him.

It's possible to be anointed with the Holy Spirit- smeared with the Holy Spirit, like having the oil poured on and rubbed in, like a spiritual massage. Then some "as it is in heaven" (Matthew 6:10 rubs off on us and we carry this realm everywhere we go. That's the anointing! The first thing that happens when the anointing touches our lives is a release of vision, strength and purpose. Our horn is exalted like the wild ox. Horn means strength.

Psalms 92:10 But my horn shalt thou exalt like *the horn of* an unicorn: I shall be anointed with fresh oil.

The first thing that happens when the anointing touches our lives is a release of vision, strength and purpose. Our horn is exalted like the wild ox. Horn means strength. When God anoints our horn, He blesses our strength, our vision, our purpose and our destiny. When God anoints our strength we want to run again – harder and faster. We're not going to let up or shut up! With the anointing we'll flourish and prosper like a palm tree.

Psalms 92:12 The righteous shall flourish like the palm tree: he shall grow like a cedar in Lebanon. This resilient tree is one of the only trees on earth that can grow in a dry and thirsty land.

We can be like a palm tree-even when it's dry and revival is over, we're still in revival and people are still getting saved and healed. In fact, people love to be around the anointing on our lives and to see the power of God in operation as people are saved, healed and delivered. The righteous shall still bear fruit in old age; they shall be fresh, fat, abundant, green and flourishing.

Psalms 92:14 They shall still bring forth fruit in old age; they shall be fat and flourishing;

Fruitfulness and freshness! That's what we want in the kingdom-to bear much fruit and to be empowered to declare the gospel and the testimony of Jesus.

John 15:16 Ye have not chosen me, but I have chosen you, and ordained you, that ye should go and bring forth fruit, and *that* your fruit should remain: that whatsoever ye shall ask of the Father in my name, he may give it you.

God is heavily on our side and wants us to have a bigger, fresher, fruitful vision. God wants us to succeed and to increase.

John 10:10 The thief cometh not, but for to steal, and to kill, and to destroy: I am come that they might have life, and that they might have *it* more abundantly.

When the anointing touches our lives, our roots will go down deep and we'll be in a good position to receive revelation from God. We can grow like a cedar (Psalms 92:12). Did you know that the cedar is one of the mightiest trees in Israel and it symbolizes spiritual maturity? We can walk in this kind of strength and anointing. As well, another secret to the anointing is discovered when we read David's description of the intensity of the anointing on his life.

Psalms 52:8 But I *am* like a green olive tree in the house of God: I trust in the mercy of God for ever and ever.

The secret is that God wants us to be in His house because these are days of intimacy and abiding in the vine. That is a key to the anointing! Remaining in the presence of God and abiding in the vine is the key to fruitfulness and much fruit that will remain.

John 15:7 If ye abide in me, and my words abide in you, ye shall ask what ye will, and it shall be done unto you. Only the friends of God, who remain in the house of God, can pray with that kind of expectation.

When we abide in the vine, the Lord's favor is upon our lives and He has great freedom to release what we need so that we can win souls! Real prosperity means having more than enough resources to do what we're called to do so that we can fulfill the vision God gave us.

You know, the Lord wants those believers who hear the call, to acquire buildings and lands so that believers have a place to receive training and equipping for the harvest. However, to prosper in this way, we also need to be out of debt so we're free to go into the nations and win the lost for Christ. God will make a way for the resources to be released to us so that we can go. In Bible times there were seasons when no one was lacking. People sold their possessions and lands, bring the proceeds and laying them at the apostle's feet so they could distribute to anyone that had need (Acts 4:34-35). Most of us would like to be in a position where people just come and bless us for the work of the ministry. We're not after the material blessing that favor brings; we're after the favor-then everything else will take care of itself.

How would you like the kind of favor that causes the Holy Spirit to come upon your life to stay? When Samuel the prophet anointed young David with golden oil to be King of Israel, the Spirit of the Lord came mightily upon him from that day on.

1 Samuel 16:13 Then Samuel took the horn of oil, and anointed him in the midst of his brethren: and the Spirit of the LORD came upon David from that day forward. So Samuel rose up, and went to Ramah.

Now that's favor! But even though David had this anointing on his life, he had to hide in caves and the wilderness with about 400 discontented men (1 Samuel 22:1-2). In contemporary terms it was the bums, robbers, misfits, drug addicts and prostitutes that came out to David in the strongholds they volunteered to serve him.

The Lord called some of the men to come and help David become King and they shared out of association, the same as David. It was a great anointing because the Spirit of the Lord came upon him mightily to stay. These men were the ones that David would be the most faithful to. These guys were saying something like this to David: We recognize that even though you're not King right now, we want to get in on ground level. We know that God has called you to be the King of Israel even though you don't look like a King at this moment, even though you're running from Saul, hiding out in the wilderness. So often, on the first glance, circumstances look one way. Yet, in reality, they aren't really the way they look! You might have one little person in your cramped office and 50 people in your church. Still, you're faithful and you're pressing through. You may not look like a King, but a few people recognize the anointing and calling on your life.

You might not have the big palace or the big ministry right now, but if you get the anointing people will want to be around it. The business men will come; the partners and the people with lands and houses will come; they will put resources at your feet. They will partner with you because the favor of the Lord is upon you.

Queen Esther certainly had favor! She was taken from the safety of her uncle's home and ushered into the royal palace when the king was looking for a new Queen it wasn't long before she obtained the favor of the official in charge then she received her beauty preparations and an allowance (Esther 2:9). Initially she spent six months in the oil, which represents death, suffering, sacrifice and dying to the flesh. That's one of the keys to the anointing. Spend as much time as possible in the oil! Then, for six months, she was treated with the perfumes the fragrance of Jesus; the presence of God.

After her preparation time she was taken to the king; he chose her to be Queen above all the other beautiful women.

Esther 2:17 And the king loved Esther above all the women, and she obtained grace and favour in his sight more than all the virgins; so that he set the royal crown upon her head, and made her queen instead of Vashti. The fact that her heritage was Jewish was never disclosed to the king. Some time later, Queen Esther answered the challenge to stand in the gap on behalf of her people because a wicked governmental official wanted to wipe them out completely. And so she presented herself to her husband, the King. And when he saw her, he asked,

Esther 5:1-3 Now it came to pass on the third day, that Esther put on *her* royal *apparel,* and stood in the inner court of the king's house, over against the king's house: and the king sat upon his royal throne in the royal house, over against the gate of the house. And it was so, when the king saw Esther the queen standing in the court, *that* she obtained favour in his sight: and the king held out to Esther the golden sceptre that *was* in his hand. So Esther drew near, and touched the top of the sceptre. Then said the king unto her, What wilt thou, queen Esther? And what *is* thy request? it shall be even given thee to the half of the kingdom.

Because she had favor with the King she could ask what she wished. However, let's not miss this: there is a crucial principle that brought this favor preparation! She prepared herself because she was hungry and desperate to find favor by calling for a fast and setting herself apart.

Esther 4:16 Go, gather together all the Jews that are present in Shushan, and fast ye for me, and neither eat nor drink three days, night or day: I also and my maidens will fast likewise; and so will I go in unto the king, which *is* not according to the law: and if I perish, I perish.

We need to be like Esther if were going to be moved into a place of ruling and reigning and finding favor. It means preparing our lives like Esther prepared her for life. She kept herself clean and pure, a virgin without spot, free from the unclean things that were in the world. She was after one thing – favor with the King.

Esther became Queen after she received favor over and above all the other women. She was the favorite! God loves each of us with an unconditional love but favor is different! God can actually favor someone more than someone else. Scripture gives us examples of favoritism: God favored Joseph above all his brothers (Genesis 37) and He also favored Jacob above Esau (Genesis 27). Why? It's because God rewards the one who is intimately acquainted with him; the one who diligently seeks Him. If we're not seeking Him as passionately as the next person, we may not have as much favor and anointing on our lives.

God responds to the heart that chases after Him, the heart like King David's. Even though, at times, David's life was a mess and he didn't walk in holiness, his heart's desire was to be right with God. That should bring encouragement to us. When we think of all the ways that we fall short, God is saying: You've had a heart that's been hungry for Me! Your heart has been hungry for My presence and you have pursued My presence. I want to reward your faithfulness. Intimacy with God brings His favor and that's where the anointing is!

It's time to search after God; to desire an intimate relationship with Him. In that place of intimacy we are prepared to receive from the hand of the Lord whatever He wishes to release. I believe the Lord wants to impart and release to us the supernatural grace called great grace. With great grace comes a fresh excitement and new level of acceleration in our walk with the Lord.

It's the supernatural grace called great grace. With great grace comes a fresh excitement and new level of acceleration in our walk with the Lord. It's the supernatural grace, power and presence that came upon the apostles of old and the early believers:

Acts 4:33 And with great power gave the apostles witness of the resurrection of the Lord Jesus: and great grace was upon them all.

This same grace and power can also be released today upon our lives. "With great power" means with miracles, signs and wonders with great anointing, "And great grace was upon the all." What brought the great grace of God? "…with great power the Apostles gave witness…" Great power brings great grace. Again great grace is the supernatural function of the Holy Spirit coming upon us to do impossible feats by the Spirit of Grace. Great Power! Great Grace! I believe that we find the first reference to this great grace in the Old Testament when the angel of the Lord referred to "grace, grace."

The angel was speaking about Zerubbabel, the man He was commissioning to rebuild the temple.

Zechariah 4:7 Who *art* thou, O great mountain? before Zerubbabel *thou shalt become* a plain: and he shall bring forth the headstone *thereof with* shoutings, *crying,* Grace, grace unto it.

The "grace, grace" needed in the rebuilding of the temple was the same "great grace" necessary for building the early church–it is also an empowerment today's church needs to prepare it for the soon–coming King. In the church today there is a growing hunger to see a multiplication of the presence, the fire, the blessing and the favor of God. Our Father wants to release opportunities, inheritance and ownership of lands and building to His children. Great grace will usher in a release of anointing for multiplication! The apostle Luke writes in Acts about how the Word of God spread and grew.

Acts 6:7 And the word of God increased; and the number of the disciples multiplied in Jerusalem greatly; and a great company of the priests were obedient to the faith.

The disciples gave themselves continually to the Word of God and prayer; then the Word of God was demonstrated and the disciples multiplied greatly. The Lord is about to release an anointing for multiplication! I'm contending for that multiplication! I'm contending for that multiplication... God took just five loaves and a few fish and multiplied it to feed 5,000 with twelve baskets left over. That's a principle in the kingdom (Luke 9:15). But there's a battle raging against the body of Christ receiving great grace because it will ring an anointing for multiplication! We often find ourselves with a dream and a vision but we're not empowered we lack what we need to do what God has called us to do. But when a little is multiplied, then resources are stretched supernaturally! Zerubbabel needed resources and manpower to rebuild the temple. He cried out: How, what, when, where, Why?!

I don't have the money! I don't have the laborers! I don't have the infrastructure! I don't have the staff! I don't have anything that I need in the natural to do what God has called me to do, but I have the dream and the vision! I don't know how to get from point A to point B! Look at how the Lord responded:
Zechariah 4:6 Then he answered and spake unto me, saying, This *is* the word of the LORD unto Zerubbabel, saying, Not by might, nor by

power, but by my spirit, saith the LORD of hosts.

He tells Zerubbabel that the answer he is searching for is found in His Spirit and in His anointing. Great power brings great grace and great grace brings great provision! Zerubbabel was looking for the stuff that the favor brings, but the favor comes out of the power and the power comes out of God's presence! It's like He's showing Zerubbabel and all of us, that the answer is symbolized and demonstrated in the golden oil dripping into the bowls (Zechariah 4:12), the ever constant, increasing flow of oil. We need the anointing! We need the power of God! Then everything will fall into place!

God is encouraging Zerubbabel, declaring that his destiny will be fulfilled; what God called him to do will be accomplished. Zerubbabel will stand in his high calling and will endure with shouts of "grace, grace" to it! We need to receive the touch of God, the fire of God and the presence of God just like Zerubbabel did. We don't need more doctrines, more papers or more licenses. God can use those things, but God can also use a poor uneducated man that has never been to a Bible school, who has received the touch of God's Spirit. It's like God is saying: It's not by might; it's not by power; it's not by staff, it's not by dollars in the bank… it's by My Spirit.

Don't let your life be hindered by what you don't have. Great power and great anointing bring great grace, which brings great provision. We all have a measure of favor, but there's more that God wants to give to us and the key to this increase is intimacy. I'm telling you, the provision of God comes from waiting for His blessing. These are days of intimacy with God; an intimacy that releases the power of God, which, in turn, releases favor. The favor of God comes by the anointing, which releases the provision of God. We can't get favor without the anointing. You can't build these into the kingdom with nothing but the anointing. By the presence and the anointing, God is building the ministry through me. It isn't my preaching that's bringing the blessing. Everything about my past disqualifies me and everything about who I am today should disqualify me. So you should be encouraged! As a minister of God, I go for it and the money comes in are budget is increasing rapidly, people don't understand how my brain works. I move forward in the presence of God, demonstrated in my life through miracles signs and wonders that's the anointing.

When believers experience Holy Ghost power, there is a release the provision the anointing of Gods grace is the word of the Lord for this hour. Grace you can receive it by faith. God is going to do something so supernatural and he is going to do it by the spirit called grace, grace. From something to nothing... grace grace. Open your heart now... the sprit of grace is about to move. God is about to touch your life anointing you with strength and taking you to the next level. Let's believe together for that anointing of great grace on our lives to extend God's kingdom on earth.

About the Author

Bill Vincent was born 12/25/73 in Illinois. Bill had a lot of challenges as a child. Bill was the teenager parents didn't want their children to hang with. Bill was invited to a prophetic service about 1990 and after he went that was the service that changed his life. Bill was born again and ministered to for the first time. The man that prophesied to Bill that day was Dennis Goodell of International Miracle Ministries. Dennis Goodell has now gone on to be with the Lord.

Bill was a servant to Dennis Goodell for about ten years and had seen and experienced a great deal of miracles. This was the man Bill received an impartation of gifts of the Holy Spirit.

Bill was trained within the Church for many years. Bill's prophetic gift was matured and sharpened. Bill was ordained in 2001 while being a minister within the Church. Bill continued ministering in the Church and other places. In 2004 Bill established a Church in Litchfield, IL.

APOSTOLIC BREAKTHROUGH

This ministry traveled as the Lord led. Bill operated in the prophetic with words of knowledge for healing spirit, soul and body. In 2008 Bill was frustrated and sought God for something fresh. After a couple of months God showed up with His mighty presence. August 2008 a Revival started. God's presence got stronger and stronger. After a few months God began to show up with mighty miracles, healing, signs and wonders. The revival continued for over two years. There were many miracles and signs every week. There were testimonies of Cancers healed, tumors removed, arthritis healed and many other creative miracles.

Bill has an accurate prophetic gift, a powerful revelatory preaching anointing with miracles signs and wonders following.

Bill started a ministry by the name of Revival Waves of Glory Ministries in 2010. This ministry is a ministry with a fresh vision. God has brought Bill through much adversity. This ministry has already had signs and wonders with deep prophetic ministry. Bill is a Prophet of God with a true Apostolic Anointing. Bill has authored many books, established a School of ministry called The School of the Supernatural and created a book publishing company called Revival Waves of Glory Books & Publishing.

Bill has found the glory of God in an awesome way. He has a special relationship with the father and powerful revelatory, healing and prophetic anointings.

Recommended Books

By Bill Vincent

Overcoming Obstacles
Glory: Pursuing God's Presence
Defeating the Demonic Realm
Increasing Your Prophetic Gift
Increase Your Anointing
Keys to Receiving Your Miracle
The Supernatural Realm
Waves of Revival
Increase of Revelation and Restoration
The Resurrection Power of God
Discerning Your Call of God
Apostolic Breakthrough
Glory: Increasing God's Presence
Love is Waiting – Don't Let Love Pass You By
The Healing Power of God
Glory: Expanding God's Presence
Receiving Personal Prophecy
Signs and Wonders
Signs and Wonders Revelations
Children Stories
The Rapture
The Secret Place of God's Power
Building a Prototype Church
Breakthrough of Spiritual Strongholds
Glory: Revival Presence of God
Overcoming the Power of Lust
Glory: Kingdom Presence of God

APOSTOLIC BREAKTHROUGH

Transitioning to the Prototype Church
The Stronghold of Jezebel
Healing After Divorce
A Closer Relationship With God
Cover Up and Save Yourself
Desperate for God's Presence
The War for Spiritual Battles
Spiritual Leadership
Global Warning
Millions of Churches
Destroying the Jezebel Spirit
Awakening of Miracles
Deception and Consequences Revealed
Are You a Follower of Christ
Don't Let the Enemy Steal from You!
A Godly Shaking
The Unsearchable Riches of Christ
Heaven's Court System
Satan's Open Doors
Armed for Battle
The Wrestler
Spiritual Warfare: Complete Collection
Growing In the Prophetic
The Prototype Church: Complete Edition
Faith
The Angry Fighter's Story
Understanding Heaven's Court System

Web Site:
www.revivalwavesofgloryministries.com

www.ingramcontent.com/pod-product-compliance
Lightning Source LLC
Chambersburg PA
CBHW030534080526
44586CB00011B/437